OF, BY, AND FOR THE HANGED MAN

A. M. PFEFFER

Royal Mast Publishing

Published by Royal Mast Publishing

Editing and book design by The Artful Editor

Paperback ISBN: 978-0-9600551-1-1
E-Book ISBN: 978-0-9600551-0-4

Printed in the United States of America

For my wife, Shannon. My leader.

And our ebullient son, Ellis "Crankenstein, Grumblefish, Wrestle Bear, Shu Shu, Booby Jooby, Strong Dog, Chooch Monster, Johnson, Moofin Stuffer, Boo Toes."

INTRODUCTION

Trainspotting. The original. 1996, in case you don't remember the year. A rather muted year by today's standards, as it were. Unless, of course, the discovery of the ancient port of Alexandria or France halting nuclear testing or even Major League Soccer making its premiere in the United States float the fuck out of your boat. But, assuming Pokémon's debut, Bill Clinton easily clinching a second term, Michael Jordan's sixth NBA championship, and Hurricane Dolly with her 80-mph winds leave you feeling a little underwhelmed, you are not alone. Then again, dig deeper and you find that some important historical gems presented themselves in that year.

"Such as?"

Such as IBM's Deep Blue becoming the first computer to win a game of chess against a reigning human champion. Such as the birth of Google at Stanford University and of Dolly the Sheep, the first mammal ever cloned from an adult somatic cell, at the University of Edinburgh. How about homegrown terrorist and noted technophobe Ted Kaczynski (the Unabomber) finally being detained after a seventeen-year manhunt? And, certainly, the formation of the first democratically elected Palestinian Parliament.

Oh, and *Trainspotting*. Absofuckinglutely, ranked ninety-seventh at the box office, *Trainspotting*.

"Yeah, great movie and all, but, uh…?"

Hold on, I'm getting nostalgic over here: *The job, the family, the fucking big television. The washing machine, the car, the compact disc and electric tin opener, good health, low cholesterol, dental insurance, mortgage, starter home, leisure wear, luggage, three-piece suit, DIY, game shows, junk food, children, walks in the park, nine to five, good at golf, washing the car, choice of sweaters, family Christmas, indexed pension, tax exemption, clearing gutters, getting by, looking ahead, the day you die.*

That's Ewan McGregor as Renton delivering the last lines of the movie.

"Cool diatribe, but that didn't exactly clear anything up for me."

No, naturally it would not. Naturally, you are left searching for clarity amid a pile of information I have thrown at you from one fantastic rant and one calendar year alone. A tepid year at that. A year nearly a quarter of a century in our past now. So, how about fast-forwarding to present day with me, if you will. Do I dare repeat the exercise using 2018?

"Oh, for the love of—*don't!*"

Painful to think how much more intense the assault on your senses, right? How much more heightened the political climate or, worse, the thought of how the actual climate can make you feel these days. How dizzying the technology. How contaminated our entertainment outlets. How intense the terrorism, the racism, the jingoism, the fanaticism have all become!

"Stop, please, I'm starting to sweat."

Well, here's the good news…it's all going to be okay.

"Is it though?"

It definitely is. Because you're going to face it all head-on AND come out better for having done so. Scratch that. You're legitimately going to come out on top for having done so. Yep, that is correct, good people, you're going to thrive in today's environment, and well into the coming decades, I might add. Going even farther out on a limb, I decree right now that you're going to savor the sweet taste of triumph over all the noise. I know this, because the Hanged Man always wins.

"Uh-huh, I mean, I'd love to bite, but about this Hanged Man?"

Sure, I get it, seems a bit morbid. Fair assessment. Except it's not at all, and that's really the point of this entire work. Pay close attention and you'll find the writing on the wall is exactly as it seems. The carpet matches the drapes. The—

"Yo, Pfeffer, maybe a little focus?"

My bad.

Some years ago, the Norse god Odin suspended himself upside down from the tree Yggdrasil so he could witness the Germanic runes in the Well of Urd and harness their cosmological powers. Right, okay, he may have been a mythological figure, but he was also an insatiable knowledge seeker, constantly in search of improvement—even sacrificing an eye to access the world-shaping force that were the runes. Odin's fable later became synonymous with that of the "the Hanged Man," a depictive figure representing paradox. More specifically, the Hanged Man is a symbol of truth in its opposite form, exemplifying contradiction. Suspend yourself upside down and you, too, can discover powerful truths in your own contradictions the likes of morality, faith, and equanimity, to name a few we are about to explore together.

"Well, that sounds kind of awesome."

It is awesome. And though this should go without saying, the dictum applies to all people from all walks of life. *Hanged Man* is all genders, including those who are gender-nonconforming. Hanged Man encompasses all races, religions, ethnicities, and creeds. Hanged Man has no limitations and makes no exclusions.

"And you've hung yourself upside down and discovered truth in your own contradictions?"

Oh, I most certainly have. Contradictions regarding tolerance, loyalty, mortality, and prosperity, to name a few more, and now I'm ever-fucking eager to share the truths discovered. Hell, I'm downright obsessive about the truth. Your truth, my truth, the whole world's truth, dammit! Because to survive and thrive as the screaming cacophony of misinformation all around us loudens by the day, the best possible perspective is required, and uncovering truth—and only truth—is needed now more than ever. The dirt-under-your-fingernails kind of truth. Vegas at 4:11 a.m. on a Wednesday truth. In the long run, gut-wrenching veracity is best revealed when the other party is a little thrown off. Or turned on. Or frightened. Or willing to let go. Just enough. Which also means, to bring about all this truth, we're gonna spar, you and I. So be on guard.

"Whoa."

Whoa, indeed. You'll forgive me for this, of course, because I'm definitely going to entertain you as well, but I simply must pick this fight with you. Maybe even more than one fight.

"How many fights, now?"

As many as it takes! Seriously, I want to know you, and that's going to require a few cracked eggs. Moreover, I want you to know ME, a walking, talking example of paradox if there ever became one, and I aim to prove the truth discovered in my contradictions will inspire you to discover your own. Which brings us to the two main components you are about to read:

- My story. More important to you, how my story relates to our larger life story as modern humans.
- All that befalls us. More important to you, how gaining the upper hand on all this befalling via a clear perspective will ultimately safeguard the survival of our species.

Simple, no? But also a tad fucking complex, yes? That's the divinity of the Hanged Man, good people. Hanged Man is paradox personified. Hanged Man is to be our representative on this journey of self-discovery, as well as a symbolic reminder that we should endlessly strive for a better world than the one we currently inhabit. One without all the misapplied divisiveness. A world where certitude is supreme, where vulnerability is a strength, and where everyone simultaneously understands that the survival of our species is what matters most.

Never lose sight of that last goal. Human existence must endure, which means we must first learn to accept our truths so that humanity can subsist long term. In other words, PROSPER TODAY so that we may PERPETUATE TOMORROW.

"This all seems...pretty damn aspirational of you."

Say it with me now: PROSPER TODAY, PERPETUATE TOMORROW. One more time. With feeling! PROSPER TODAY, PERPETUATE TOMORROW. Give me the chance, and I will demonstrate for you that Hanged Man lights the best way onward. I will demonstrate contradiction—specifically our own contradictions—are imperative to ensuring our species continues a long life on this planet. I will prove that should we ourselves succeed in Prospering Today, we will all positively Perpetuate Tomorrow.

Remember 1996?

"Sure do, it was only, like, five pages ago."

But do you really remember 1996? One of the worst blizzards in U.S. history killed more than 150 people along the Eastern Seaboard. A truck filled with explosives injured over fourteen hundred people during a bank bombing in Colombo, Sri Lanka. Sixteen infant pupils and one teacher were killed in Scotland by a lone gunman. More than a hundred Lebanese civilians died from errant Israeli shelling during what came to be known as the Qana Massacre. Hurricane Bertha made "rare" landfall in North Carolina. The Taliban first caught the world's attention upon capturing Kabul, the capital city of Afghanistan. Ethiopian Airlines Flight 961 was hijacked, and all 125 people onboard died when the plane crashed into the ocean. A domestic pipe bombing terrorized the summer Olympics held in Atlanta. The insanely talented Tupac Shakur was ruthlessly gunned down. And JonBenet Ramsey was found beaten and strangled in her family's home, setting off one of the most sensational media frenzies ever televised.

So, 1996 was tepid? There is nothing tepid about any year. There is no Golden Age, when life was simpler. When terror and the climate and racial tensions and politics and monetary disparity and entertainment were less obtrusive. Yet, assuredly, important gems occur annually that advance society as well.

"Am I crazy, or did you already just blow my mind a little?"

Stick around. Seriously though, the right perspective will produce a better human timeline moving forward—one that guarantees we all thrive together. As thrive is what we aspire to. Thrive we must! Hanged Man is here to ensure all that thriving. To ensure victory above all else. Hanged Man Prospers Today so that we will all Perpetuate Tomorrow. Let us begin.

CHAPTER ONE
A BUDDHIST HUSTLER

It's essential we understand each other right away, so know this, I am not a Buddhist. At least not a purposefully practicing Buddhist or someone who ever intends to convert to Buddhism. The concept of religion aside for a moment, I want to reiterate that I have no formal allegiance to the Buddha, his teachings, or any of the five hundred million or so disciples who follow the path. I do, however, love Thai food, sans even the slightest hint of spice whatsoever, which should tell you absolutely everything and nothing about me all at once.

Shit, I was where again?

"Buddhism?"

Bless up! Four of the most vital books in my life invoke the dharma. The first of which you could prob—

"Hey! Slow down a second, please. The dharma?"

Good point, I should explain that. Though, this doesn't count as one of our fights, by the way. Also, we'll be moving nice and fast quite often. But just this one time for you, my friends...

Buddhism. Two major branches are recognized, Theravada and Mahayana. Mahayana translates to "the Great Vehicle." Theravada to "the School of the Elders." Both share the same goal to overcome suffering in this life, followed by the cycle of death and rebirth through Nirvana, or the path to Buddhahood. Annnnnnnd, I'm seeing now that this may be even more confusing than adducing the word *dharma* in the first place. Let's try this again.

Buddhism. There are four Noble Truths:

1. Suffering
2. The Cause of Suffering
3. The End of Suffering
4. The Path

You are destined to a cycle of rebirth until you can embrace and master these truths, ultimately achieving Nirvana, or the path to Buddhahood. Also, though I sportively mentioned Thai food earlier, and though over 95 percent of Thailand does follow the Theravada branch, Buddhism began in India and originated as an Indian religion. Dharma is a major concept of Indian religions (those being Hinduism, Buddhism, Jainism, and Sikhism). However, there is no single-word translation for *dharma* in Western languages, yet with regard to Buddhism, *dharma* often signifies *cosmic law and order*. It is also one of the Three Jewels of Buddhism, where practitioners take refuge. The other two jewels are the Buddha and sangha (the overall community of Buddhists). We cool? Good.

As I was saying, four of the most vital books in my life invoke the dharma. The first is a classic Buddhist novel. Yep, you knew it, *Siddhartha* by Hermann Hesse. *I shall learn from myself, be a pupil of myself, I shall get to know myself, the mystery of Pfeffer*. Fine, swap out *Siddhartha* for my surname and you just landed on the book's thesis. Page forty-seven, by the way, though I strongly suggest reading all one hundred fifty-two pages. Worth it.

The second and third books are *Sapiens* and *Homo Deus,* written by Yuval Noah Harari. And though perfectly happy to tell you how secular he is, Harari does little to hide his affinity for Buddhism in his literature. I am not complaining. And, finally, *Man's Search for Meaning*, by Viktor E. Frankl. I came by this absolute taker of breath via a therapist I visited in my early thirties. He was himself a Buddhist, and though I suspected I'd be seeing a more conventional analyst when we first began our sessions, I was pleasantly thrown off guard by his unconventional treatments and eventual conclusions about myself. Anyway, Frankl's book details his experience as an Auschwitz prisoner who survived by using his own psychotherapeutic methods of positive thinking. Behind those methods was a deep, intense, and calculated understanding that everyone suffers, so fucking own it. Own your own suffering! Buddhism at its core. Or, at least, the Buddhism at my core.

Hustling is another belief alive and well at my core. Perhaps even quite a bit more than Buddhism. I can see when I said the term *hustler,* it instantly conjured an image of a billiards shark or a three-card Monte maven or even a purveyor of cheap sidewalk hand jobs, if you will. No, I lack all those skill sets, I'm afraid, but I am no less a proud hustler. Proud. Hustler.

The preferred term in slick magazine apps these days may be *entrepreneur*, but that's not my preference. Entrepreneurs *purposefully take on greater-than-normal financial risks* to fulfill their business dreams. Why people today so eagerly label themselves financial risk takers and piss their money away is a worrying symptom of the massive malady that has threatened our fragile economic ecosystem since the Great Recession a decade ago. Take note, good people: mislabeled entrepreneurship is a frightening indicator of just how far off base we've drifted as a whole. Hence, I prefer the exact fucking opposite, thanks anyway. Day by day, month by month, good old-fashioned hustle. Aggressive enterprise at its best.

"But wait! All the online dictionaries suggest being a hustler means you are employing fraudulent or unscrupulous methods of obtaining money."

Eat shit, I say!

The first and true definition of a hustler is *an enterprising person determined to succeed.* In better words, a go-getter. The supplemental definitions are all informal colloquialisms. And though street slang can be wonderful as a communicative art, short-form slang can be dangerous. Argot is lazy, indeed, informal, and there is nothing informal about me. Just as there is nothing informal about the essence of hustle. Like everyone, I suffer. But unlike everyone, I own it, and then I hustle. Oh, do I hustle. I am, by my own anointing, a Buddhist Hustler.

Come with me back to September 2008. You remember that joyous month and year, right? Lehman Brothers filed for bankruptcy on the fifteenth, insurance giant AIG received an $85 billion cash infusion from the government on the sixteenth, and the Dow Jones plummeted like a beaten-to-shit boxer on the seventeenth when the money market funds lost $144 billion. Then the twentieth brought us the first attempt at a bailout package, which was ultimately voted down by the U.S. Senate on the twenty-ninth. The Dow Jones fell again that day, the most in a single day in history up until that time. Further back now…

Because it will explain why I'm explaining any of this. In 2004, after a string of three fantastic jobs that had me ascending the Hollywood industry ladder, the fourth one never materialized, and I found myself unemployed, penniless, and suffering gross bodily malfunctions I wouldn't know were symptoms of a vexing ailment called reactive arthritis for nearly another decade. My parents were begging me to leave Los Angeles behind, get healthy, and come work with my father and brother in the family business in Denver, Colorado. As if, *padres*, right?

"Good. Didn't take you for a milksop."

Milksop? Yeah, maybe let me do the insulting here.

Depleted in every sense of the word, I was saved from having to move back home by a college buddy who took me in, and I started scraping by with traveling notary work for many other friends and acquaintances who had found their way into the wonderful world of subprime lending as loan officers. I'll answer your immediate question as to why I didn't just become a loan officer myself since at the time jobs were available to anyone with a pulse and vocal cords… because I was still holding on to the notion that I could break back into Hollywood as either a writer or a producer, so fringe notary work at three hundred a pop was just fine by me, thank you very much.

"Come again? Did you really just say $300 a pop?"

I did, and I meant it.

You see, back then, traveling notary work to ensure loan documents were signed properly wasn't exactly like getting a one-time stamp from the guy or gal posted up at your local UPS outlet. This was a position of trust for many loan officers, who dispatched me within a twenty-five-mile radius of Los Angeles to make sure I returned with a completed (more importantly, a 100 percent correctly completed) set of loan docs that were absolutely going to fund, hence a stupidly fat commission check for the officer. Also, did I say twenty-five-mile radius? 'Cause there was that one time I drove over a hundred miles to Bakersfield for a midnight loan signing with a borrower who was leaving the country for many weeks the following day. Not shady at all. Seriously, not one iota.

And what the hell is reactive arthritis, right? It was previously known as Reiter's syndrome, but apparently eponymous Hans

Conrad Julius Reiter being a Nazi sympathizer is a bad look for WebMD, so now, reactive arthritis. Basically, it's an autoimmune response to an untreated bacterial infection. As in, food or sex bacteria. I was in my early twenties living in Los Angeles, so I'll let you imagine which of these I most likely contracted. It mostly affects men, and it often dissipates after a few months, though in a small percentage of unlucky patients the symptoms can persist for years. I am one of those unlucky patients. Don't let me bitch too much about this because it's all manageable and much better now, but it was simply astounding how many doctors and specialists had me taking test after test without ever so much as mentioning this syndrome. Finally, one doctor knew right away, when a twist of fate had me switching general practitioners and I simply explained my medical history again. Big sigh. Huge Buddhist fucking sigh. Still…

I was treading water but was so sure my life was heading in a better direction. My health had improved, and my college buddy and I had become great friends, so we decided to move to Santa Monica in search of quality ocean air and a fresh lease on life. It was also right around the time I caught what seemed to be a lucky break in my writing endeavors.

My writing partner and I had written a television show idea on spec called *HOOD*: *overindulgent trust funder partying his way across Europe is called back home to New York City when his father dies suspiciously. Dad's ruthless business partner cuts off all the money and steals our hero's claim to the family fortune for himself, aside from one vacant tenement in Harlem that Dad left our hero in a secret will.* This is the rudimentary story of Robin Hood, by the way, and our hero (damned right we named him Robin) moves into the tenement and starts helping squatters while simultaneously piecing together what really happened to dear old Dad.

Yeah, we thought it was a pretty good show idea, too, thanks for your support. Tim Story (director of the original *Barbershop*) and his development executive liked it as well, so the exec decided to work with us on it to see whether they could get it in shape for Fox TV to turn into an actual television show. Didn't happen. But what did happen is that this all came together at the same time Tim agreed to direct *Fantastic Four (Part 2)* for Fox Studios, except this time around, he could pick his own writers, since last time around he had to come in and rescue Part 1 when the original director dropped out.

You see where this is going, and it was clear those writers would be us, because we were young and malleable and cheap. Dirt cheap, in fact, as in free, because the studio hadn't signed off on us yet, and they wanted us to write a few drafts to prove our mettle. And even though we started signing talent agency and attorney representation to protect us and ultimately make sure we got paid, that's not quite what happened either.

At the very same time we started crafting our version of the script, Fox hired Mark Frost, who had written the first one and was a known commodity. He got paid a million dollars. That's not even hyperbole. That's exactly what he got paid, while my partner and I worked for free for months on a competing script. The big day finally rolled around, and both Frost's and our scripts were delivered to the studio at the same time. We won! Totally fucking kidding. That's not what happened at all. Fox hated both scripts because, well, both scripts sucked. Frost simply took his money and moved on with his life; there was no such coinage for us. If we wanted to stay on, we'd have to go back to the drawing board, while Fox hired another competing writer, Don Payne, who had just written *My Super Ex-Girlfriend* for the studio. Hollywood is a fickle mistress, my friends.

What would you have done? Your dream is to be a writer and producer, a big freaking opportunity is staring you in the face, and you don't have an advanced degree to fall back on. Your representatives are telling you to keep pushing forward, and the development exec who is spending just as much time crafting the story as you are is undoubtedly fighting with the powers that be on your behalf.

"I would have kept on writing."

We're already seeing eye to eye! Draft after draft after draft. Nearly a year of writing and rewriting, false starts, and ever-changing studio storyline notes. But looking back, it was all second-, third-, and fourth-hand information, and it occurs to me now how naive we were. Never once did we meet with a Fox studio exec, and everything was filtered through Tim's development exec. The exec was a hell of a nice guy and tremendous at his job, no doubt, but Tim was always too busy to sit down with us himself. Or, worse, he always knew we wouldn't be the winning script and was smart enough not to waste his personal time. One afternoon we were unceremoniously told it was over for us, and we never made a dime. To this day I still haven't watched *Fantastic Four: Rise of the Silver Surfer*, though I'm sure it's just a lovely little piece of celluloid.

Now it's early 2006 and I'm worse than broke, I'm in fucking debt. During the entire *Fantastic Four* desolation I continued to notarize loan documents, but I also added in loan origination to help get by.

"You know I'm going to need loan origination explained, right?"

Way ahead of you.

A few of the loan officers I was notarizing for were already, or had become, close friends, and they were making piles of dough during the subprime lending boom. But to acquire most clients meant cold calling, or "dialing for dollars," as it was affectionately known in chop shop lending circles. Not the most fun and exciting way to spend one's time, so a loan officer would often employ an intern of sorts to do the initial cold call, and if that "originator" got a bite on the line, the loan officer would take over the call and try to close the client. If the loan closed, then the originator would make a tidy fee just for opening the door. Hence my life as an originator.

But when your head and your heart are really in one place, it's difficult to be successful in another. Notary and origination work were part-time, and I was treating writing like a full-time position, which meant living on credit.

"Well, that was dumb."

Oh yes. Indubitably dumb. But please don't misconstrue how dumb it really was. To us, *Fantastic Four 2* was supposed to be the jumping-off point to a great career, so it wasn't the only writing we were doing. We were scribing feature and television spec scripts at the same time we were working on the movie, and taking meetings with any other producers or executives who may have been interested in having us write for them. It's just that those meetings and other masterpieces we were convinced would bring us fame and fortune, well, didn't. We cycled through managers as fast as we were cycling through storylines. My partner and I fought each other. A shit ton. Bills mounted; my girlfriend at the time pitied and my roommate worried for me. Winter turned into spring, which all too quickly turned into summer, or as much as seasons could turn into each other when Los Angeles feels like the loneliest fucking place on earth. Bad scripts, bad meetings, bad mojo. Fuckety fuck, fuck, fuck. Crapola!

On the contrary, the Los Angeles real estate market was on fire in 2006, with prices going up by the month. All my friends in the lending business were making gobs of what some might refer to as "funny money." This motivated me to become a full-time loan officer myself—much less than you might think, but I admit it certainly wasn't a deterrent. I officially jumped in, which was relatively easy since I already had knowledge of the industry as a notary and originator. Two of my peripheral friends (friends of friends) had opened their own lending brokerage together, and they were keen to fill chairs in their newly leased office. I signed up for my real estate salesperson's license, and it didn't take long before I had a solid pipeline of my own loans. By the end of this year I had closed enough business to pay off all my credit card debt and really think about what my future could and should look like.

We're pausing here for a moment—'cause we're going a little fast, even for my taste, and we need to briefly talk about subprime lending because it is not something to be glossed over just to keep running my mouth about myself like an asshole. To claim that these loans were specifically responsible for the global economic meltdown that occurred in September 2008 is an understatement. I was there on the front lines of this catastrophe, and they were truly the shit stains that soiled the fabric at its root, impossible ever to completely cleanse.

"Well, what about the ratings agencies like Moody's or the predators who invested Grandma's retirement portfolio into toxic debt just to make a dirty buck or the architects of collateralized debt obligations themselves?"

True, all that fucked-up shit played a pivotal part, no doubt, but those were all akin to particulate stains. Enzymatic stains. Subprime lending was pure grease. And good fucking luck getting oil out of your clothing. I ask you to think about the notion for a moment. These subprime loans were made to borrowers whose credit was already questionable—and then brokers and banks directed them to state their job descriptions and salaries to acquire a loan on their primary residence. Yep. Borrowers procuring mortgages on houses when they shouldn't have even qualified for a loan on a corndog; and the organizations who were supposed to be making sure the borrowers were truly qualified helped them make it look like they were instead! That's real-life scary. Way scarier than that clown from *It* scary.

Worse, this didn't happen a handful of times spread out among a handful of reputable lenders. A gigantic slice of the banking industry was DEDICATED to this practice. And I specifically mention primary residences because it's important to understand the mind-set it takes to justify this malfeasance. Blame who you will for what ultimately happened: Wall Street, the banks, the brokers, the borrowers; that's up to you, but it was all perpetrated upon the one societal foundation that has been sold as the American Dream: homeownership.

Equity in the homes we live in was used to finance anything and everything we could get our grubby little hands on. *The homes we live in.* Eat in. Sleep in. Fuck in. Grow up in. Share our lives in! The erosion of the middle class took a gigantic leap forward when this all went down.

Of course, I won't pretend I had any idea at the time I was slinging these mortgages of what was to come. I am no Michael J. Burry (*The Big Short* is a fantastic book and movie), but I can defend my conscience just a little bit here. Much to the chagrin of my company superiors, I left a lot of money on the table as a loan officer in late 2006 and the first part of 2007 by pushing certain loan products that were slightly more beneficial to the borrower than to me, the loan officer. But let's not let me fool you too much. I am not entitled to sainthood and expect no medals here. I notarized, originated, and personally closed my fair share of crappy loans and helped a few too many people leverage home equity for all the wrong reasons. So, if you currently feel like punching me in the abdomen, I understand.

"You dastardly son of a bitch!"

[Taking a bow]

Before you think I got away with anything, though, none of this lasted very long. Okay, that whole paragraph about lost billions and bailout packages in September 2008? We're back there now. And though most people might recall that month as zero hour for the global economic meltdown, to those of us in the fucked-up subprime world, the writing was on the wall in the middle of 2007 when the funders started burping.

"Um, maybe in layperson's English please, schmuck."

A bit touchy, yet probably appropriately so at this point.

Brokers exist because they can get wholesale interest rates from certain banks that borrowers cannot get directly from those banks. Plus, brokers know best how to package loan applications for those banks to get borrowers funded. During the subprime days, those banks had names like Downey, Fremont, and World Savings. Never heard of them? That's okay, they don't exist anymore, but they were big in the late nineties and early aughts. And when I say they started to "burp," I mean that many of their loans began going sour when the real estate market finally reached its apex and there was no more room for anyone's home equity to keep going up, up and up some more. Late monthly payments turned into fully defaulted loans, which ultimately turned into foreclosures. Shit was bad if you were a broker because these wholesale lines started drying up since said banks were taking on waves of foreclosures and had to halt their lending programs. I picked a great time to finally enter the industry, *n'est-ce pas?* But wait, it gets worse.

Right around the same time that I started doing well, I had grown tight with one of the owners of the brokerage I was working at (along with one other loan officer) and we decided we were going to be millionaire real estate investors too.

"Oy."

Hey, blow it out your ass! But also, yeah, oy.

We devised a plan to buy out-of-state rental properties for cash, fix them up, re-rent them, refinance them—AND the cash we would pull back out would not only cover the costs of purchase and rehab but also put extra money in our pockets. AND we would still be making enough in rents to cover the debt service and all other expenses. The amazing thing is that this works for real estate investors all the time. It's just that you should really know what you're doing to employ this method correctly. Alas, we did not.

I'm not ashamed of much in my life—after all, one with an affinity for Buddhism shouldn't be. But I am thoroughly ashamed to say we landed on Syracuse, New York, as our investment farm because we read an article in *USA Today* that pointed to Syracuse as a good city for real estate investment. Not kidding. *US-fucking-A Today*. It still sends chills down my spine thinking about this. Okay, here goes.

It took a few months to locate target properties in Syracuse… you know what? Strike that from the record. We didn't really locate the properties ourselves. What actually happened was we came upon a local investor in Syracuse who was getting properties under contract and selling the contracts to neophyte investors like us for an assignment fee. This is not a novel concept and is known as "wholesaling" in the real estate investment world. But at the time, to us, it became known as "paying retail price for shitboxes in an absolutely terrible part of town."

Also, we never even went to Syracuse to see the inventory we were buying. We simply purchased properties sight unseen. I know, I know, please stop yelling at me. Worse, don't forget that though the internet was advanced around this time, websites like Zillow and Trulia had just launched, so we didn't even have good pictures to go by. That's the thing about hustlers, we often lead with our hearts, not with our heads.

Yeah, I hear myself. Calm the fuck down.

We quickly acquired our first three properties, and all of them were major pains in the ass, even with property managers handling the rehabs and tenancies. We were hemorrhaging money and not at all refinancing for more than we were in them for. But we weren't yet worried because we were still closing loans at this point, so what was a few extra dollars to stabilize our new rental portfolio? Except, yeah, then the subprime banks started burping.

"Yoinks."

Tell me about it, Scooby-Doo.

We were officially chickens with our heads cut off by the end of that year, running out of lenders to originate subprime loans with while convincing ourselves that we could become full-time real estate investors and leave mortgage brokering behind. This is exactly what we did. When I say "we," I mean that the partner of the brokerage split up with his partner to become my partner, along with the other loan officer I mentioned, and we went off together to lease a much smaller office space and focus on acquiring more rental units. Cripes, this is painful!

So, after a few more acquisitions in Syracuse, we turned our focus to Saint Louis, Missouri, for pretty much the same reason we chose Syracuse. We had zero fucking idea what we were doing. More buying from wholesalers at terribly inflated retail prices, more sourcing property managers who abused the hell out of out-of-state landlords, and more inventory purchased sight unseen. And, yes, now the rest of the world is starting to take notice of a real problem with foreclosures by the springtime of this year. Then another summer came around.

Oh, the shitshow that was the summer of 2008.

In the early part of that season, we were burning through cash at an alarming rate. We had something like eleven properties in all, including one in Riverside, California, that we purchased with the intent to flip and that was a whole other headache I'll spare you having to get even angrier with me about.

"Too late."

Right, well, it became clear every month brought a new, unforeseen expenditure and our tenants liked destroying our units more than they liked paying rent. And since we were no longer brokering subprime loans and not refinancing back out as much as we planned for our "salaries," any personal savings we had was gone and I was back to racking up credit card debt. Okay, fine, I also began racking up personal loan debt, since banks were still giving those out; I had even leveraged my car to 125 percent face value because that's how fucking ridiculous the lending world had become!

The middle of that summer was a fever dream. Part hallucinogenic nightmare, part heart-thumping lucidity, and all never-ending math. Previous life fights with parents, girlfriends, teachers...they had nothing on the fights I was having with my investment partners. Sweet times.

I finally flew to New York in July, borrowed a car from my brother who was living in NYC, and drove up to Syracuse to meet with our property manager to assess the situation. The company was a local landlord itself that owned a ton of functioning units around town, and I still appreciate them taking me out for a pity meal and putting a sirloin in my belly before walking me to the gallows the next day.

My friends, it was fucking brutal. We had three triplexes and a quadplex, and half of the units were either vacant or so beat to crap from the previous tenant they were uninhabitable. The money it would take to fix them up for the umpteenth time wasn't going to be worth it, and it was clear the real estate bubble had officially popped and banks (and I mean all the banks in the world) were in crisis mode. I went back to my Red Robin Inn that night, most likely masturbated while crying, then called my partners. We all agreed it was time to fire sale whatever property we were holding.

August was…eventful? No, not quite right. Traumatic? Not quite cutting it either. Superfuckingcalefragapocalyptic? There it is. We were able to unload a grand total of two properties, which meant the others would have to be dealt with later. As I was completely tapped out of funds, my parents were again begging me to leave Los Angeles to get my life together. Instead, I convinced them to let me borrow a few bucks so I could stay in LA, create a little financial cushion, and ultimately eat something other than lint for the rest of the year. I informed my disappointed roommate that I would be moving out end of September and began looking for a bartending job as soon as I got back from New York. And though I had previous experience as a mixologist, this was not an easy gig to get in a city like Los Angeles, let me tell you.

Amid uncorking the failing real estate venture with my partners, selling off most of my life's possessions, letting all personal debts go into default for the first time ever, figuring out where I was going to live next without any money coming in, knocking on doors for a bartending job daily, and wallowing in my mistakes, I did manage to do something prescient.

Some little voice inside kept screaming that any future success for me rested solely on putting previously used shortcuts behind me. If I was being totally honest with myself (which is clearly why we have gathered here today), I was that guy who bullshitted his way through everything, and that had to stop. Pronto. So, while all the life cleaning was taking place day by day, I found a few minutes to hang my salesperson's license with Keller Williams Realty on Sunset Strip in Hollywood.

This was not because I wanted to be a realtor at all, but it was because that little voice was telling me that if I ever wanted to be a true real estate investor, I needed to, you know, effectively learn something about the real estate industry.

"Makes sense. But what abou—"

You want me to explain this salesperson's license I keep mentioning, don't you?

"How'd you know?"

Lucky guess.

To negotiate either realty or loan transactions, you must be licensed by a Department of Real Estate (at least in California that's how it works). And when you complete the required courses and take the state test, you get a salesperson's license, which you then hang under a licensed broker. My partner who ran the mortgage company was a broker, and he relinquished his title as my specific broker, so I could then hang my license where I pleased, and I chose Keller Williams Realty.

This would prove fortuitous because, when I was physically at the Comedy Store on Sunset Boulevard one day in dropping off a résumé for the bartender position, I got a call from a good friend I'd been hitting up for weeks about a job at the Sunset Marquis Hotel where he was a night manager. Well, he just came through in a big way and told me I needed to get there fast. Of all days

I could get this call, I mean, I was literally around the corner. I raced down to meet with the general manager and tried my best to come off as humble and confident at the same time, as this was now my last hope of staying in Los Angeles. It must have worked, because he hired me on the spot and expected me to start the next day.

"That's a hell of a good interview!"

And then some.

Anyway, by chance, the Keller Williams office I had already hung my license with was across the street from the hotel. As in, directly across Alta Loma Boulevard, just south of Sunset Boulevard. And since I'd be working the restaurant bar, my shift would be four in the afternoon to around midnight every night. Why is that important? Because unlike most bartending jobs that last until two in the morning, followed by cleanup and shutdown, so more like three a.m., I could still go to bed at a decent hour. That meant getting up early enough each next day to figure out how to jumpstart my real estate career. The thought was: get up, go to the KW office and learn all day, bartend all night, settle my debts as fast as possible, then get back to real estate investing permanently.

I was twenty-nine years old when I signed my employee agreement with the Sunset Marquis. Eight years removed from a marketing degree from Indiana University's Kelley School of Business and about eight fucking minutes removed from packing it all in to go live in my parents' basement with my tail planted firmly between my legs.

The following month was one of the craziest I can remember.

For starters, I think I worked something like sixteen days in a row at the bar before taking a day off. Naturally, laws in place since the Industrial Revolution prohibit that kind of exhaustive overload, but I'm not complaining. At all. I was so thankful to even have a job, let alone an immediate cash tips job, that I loved every second. Plus, it was fair to say that I was a little rusty from the last time I had been a bartender (ten years prior at a neo-Nazi biker bar behind Coors Field in Denver).

"Wait, what?!"

Perhaps a story for another book, we've got a lot more to cover here...

Sixteen straight days because I really needed the extra work to fine-tune my mixology game. I mean, it wasn't like there were times someone would order something only to find me quickly darting into the backroom and Googling how to make their order. Fine, you got me again, it was exactly like that! You know what? We're going a little fast once more. Let's talk about the Sunset Marquis because it needs to be talked about and you need the visual.

In a world where just about everything has been corporatized, the Sunset Marquis Hotel remains one of the last great bastions of family-owned real estate to this day. In 1960, developer George Rosenthal cold-called Hugh Hefner and pitched him an idea to build a Los Angeles Playboy Club on the famed Sunset Strip and at the same time to also build an adjacent Playboy Hotel to house guests and entertainers. Hefner was in, but community backlash nearly forced them to accept a $12 million loan from Jimmy Hoffa as the only way to fund the enterprise. Not too excited about being indebted to the mafia, they smartly balked at the last minute, and Rosenthal secured financing from local lenders to build the Playboy club and offices, but not the hotel. Undeterred, he began erecting the club and settled on plans for a much smaller hotel after purchasing land directly off Sunset Boulevard. The hotel ultimately opened before the club did, in 1963, and it was the first all-suite hotel in the United States. Then the club opened on New

Year's Eve, 1964, and true to the plan, the hotel, consisting mostly of private villas and junior suites, operated as an apartment hotel to service the offices and club.

A little confusing? What's not confusing is why the hotel long outlasted the club. It became a preeminent destination for huge celebrities, specifically rock-and-roll stars from around the world. Both the lure and allure of the hotel were irresistible to music insiders. The 1960s housed the Playboy entertainment. The first half of the 1970s brought through eclectic rock pioneers such as Bruce Springsteen, Bob Marley, and Elton John. The late seventies gave way to punk and new wave mainstays like The Clash, Joan Jett, and The Ramones. The eighties were all about metal and big hair, and where do you think most of them stayed when they came through Los Angeles? Tremendous guess. Then, as music became more diversified in the 1990s, so too did the hotel.

Rande Gerber was a big-shot entertainment mogul who found massive success with the Whiskey Blue in New York City, so the Sunset Marquis formed an alliance with him to bring that same vibe to the hotel bar (not to be confused with the Whisky A Go-Go). That vibe, simply put, was raucous sex and drugs. Don't get this wrong, there was already plenty of that going on at the hotel for decades, but not all of it was at that extra level of raucous until The Whiskey Bar reveled in such behavior. Typhoon-level debauchery on some evenings, I've been told. And at about the same time Gerber was lighting up the hotel lobby night after night, something else very cool was being born down in the basement.

Jed Leiber is the son of Jerry Leiber, one of the great songwriters in early rock-and-roll history. He gave Elvis "Hound Dog" and "Jailhouse Rock." The Drifters got "Fools Fall in Love" and "There Goes My Baby." Ben E. King got "Stand by Me." You get the idea. Anyway, his son Jed was (is) no slouch himself in the musical department, having crushed it as a writer and producer. One night, he and living legend Jeff Beck were in a hotel room working through a tune when the general manager started getting noise complaints from other guests (if you can believe noise complaints would even be an issue at the Marquis). So, the GM offers up a laundry room underneath the hotel next to the valet-parked cars, where Leiber and Beck could rock out to their hearts' content. Ever the hustler himself, Leiber saw an opportunity and pitched the hotel management on creating a studio space right where that laundry room was. Presto. *Nightbird Studios* is born—a state-of-the-art recording atelier and ginormous haven for Grammy-winning albums over the last twenty-five years.

"This place really exists?!"

[Nodding head vigorously]

Let's recap a moment, shall we? Even if music does not move you to your soul the way it does me, let it be known that the Sunset Marquis is a living and breathing entity unto itself. It is palpitating, tangible harmony. The Hyatt House off the Sunset Strip in Los Angeles was another mythological rock-and-roll hotel, but its lore is exemplified mostly by its excess. The Marquis is more than that. The Marquis is at once dazzlingly regal and obscenely tawdry, and often both in the course of a single night. It is not owned by SBE or Delaware North Companies or Tracinda Corporation or any other number of diluted holding companies. It is owned by the Rosenthal family. It is omnipresent melody even on its worst day. It is glory.

Annnnnnnnnd we're back: early September 2008. I am for the moment still living in Santa Monica and whittling down my possessions to whatever will fit in my car, because my plan is to couch surf for as long as possible while stockpiling as much cash as possible for wherever I landed next. It's interesting—I sold a few things, but I remember just giving away the rest. Television, bed, clothing. I distinctly remember how underwhelmed I was by my own possessions. As in, I'm twenty-nine, and this is what I've amassed? That's it? Yikes, somebody just take all this childish shit, please.

In the morning I would get into Keller Williams by nine or ten, since I was slow rolling the learning process as opposed to rushing into the unknown as I had previously. This meant mostly taking internal classes to learn the machinations of realty. On the surface, realty is relatively pedestrian, but behind the curtain lies a methodical level of organization and marketing I needed to fully grasp. This included disclosures, appraisals, title reports, insurances, software, farming systems, internal brokerage checklists, to name a few. Whereas the old me would have glossed over these elements (which is what I did with the subprime loans), the new me was digesting them all on a molecular level. But when four o'clock rolled around? I'd gladly head to the Marquis, change into the uniform, set up my station, and let the bartender in me have some fucking fun. Now as for why I was able to land this job…

After decades of municipal red tape, the Rosenthal family was finally successful in expanding the hotel beyond the villas, junior suites, lobby bar, and one centralized pool. What was added is an unexpected oasis of private luxury directly off the Sunset Strip. The hotel boasted massive new contemporary villas, a more family-friendly pool, and a centralized restaurant complete with outdoor seating and garden alcove. Then there is the bar. It's not much to look at, but I started to appreciate the design the more I worked behind it.

There are only five stools for patrons because it's really a service bar for the restaurant, and the lone bartender is tasked with fixing cocktails and supplying servers with wine as needed. It sits outside of the indoor dining portion, off to the side of the outdoor patio, as well as a good twenty feet away from the secluded garden alcove. It also is directly across from the hotel spa, which neighbors the presidential suite. Last, though still off to the side, the bar is somewhat of a gateway fixture on the pathway to the new villas. It is itself unobtrusive and yet the most focal element of the expansion all at once. It is a very good bar.

My first day on the job wasn't really that hard. The restaurant had already been through its grand opening stages, so it was not an immediate dinner hit the way it was for breakfast or lunch, which I was not on shift for. On my first shift, I basically just served a few gin and tonics to hotel guests who were looking to get loose before heading out for the night.

"What about your second shift?"

Exactly the right question. The second day...

After pulling my needed alcohol for the evening, I got back to my station to find an intricate photo shoot with Mischa Barton happening right at the foot of the bar. And it's not like anyone told me this was planned or on any schedule or anything. This was just normal Hollywood hotel life, apparently. A few hours later, with only a smattering of patrons eating in the restaurant and no one sitting at any of my stools, two unintelligible French dudes wearing the gaudiest leather jackets you've ever seen strolled up and ordered an insanely expensive bottle of champagne. They nattered away for about five minutes, then out of nowhere fifty people mobbed the pathway between the bar and the villas, including paparazzi and ten scantily dressed female models. I had no idea what the hell was going on. Christian Audigier (someone had to tell me it was him) appeared in the middle of the entire mess, and the photographers snapped pictures of him and all the models. As fast as they all appeared was as fast as they disappeared. Again, no one alerted me, and ten minutes later it was as if there had never been an impromptu Ed Hardy pajama party for no reason whatsoever. All was quiet, and I was back to making martinis for the young couple sharing a romantic night out at table six.

And then the world blows up! All people can talk about is the economic meltdown, and I'm just hoping this job doesn't suddenly disappear on me. Meanwhile, the creepy creditor calls have begun (since I let everything except my car payment go into default), but at least I officially landed a couch to stay on for a few weeks. September rolled into October, and October rolled into November, and truth be told, it was a little bleak at the bar. The expansion hadn't caught on with the Marquis clientele yet, or couldn't really, as the global financial crisis was in full swing. Then again, if I'm painting a picture of dire soup lines, I'm absolutely painting the wrong picture. This was Hollywood after all, and there were plenty of busy days and nights, especially on the weekends.

I had few possessions to speak of, I was in crippling debt and considering a bankruptcy filing since I was still personally responsible for some Syracuse mortgages, and my family was none too thrilled with my decision to stay in Tinseltown. Still, I was learning a fair amount about realty by day and learning a hell of a lot about life at night, so it wasn't all bad. I even began sourcing potential property buyers because, yes, a few were excited that the real estate market had turned, which meant good deals could be found.

"I love a good deal!"

Don't we all.

By January you might even say the mojo was making a solid comeback. Five months into Keller Williams and I was seeing dividends, with a few potential clients on my roster. And five months into the hotel service industry I started to feel a little like the *Fla-*

mingo Kid. I had the joint wired, people. I was earning the serving staff's respect, my managers liked me, as did the food runners, the hosts and hostesses, the front desk crew, the bellhops, the butler (yes, the hotel has a butler), the spa personnel—even the other bartenders on staff. They all quickly became like family. A weird-as-all-hell, slightly dysfunctional, never-fucking-boring family.

Hotel business was even starting to pick up, because a little something called Awards Season was rolling into view. Starting with the Golden Globes all the way to the Academy Awards, we would have a string of private events and plenty of nominated clientele come stay with us. And as you might imagine, the Grammys were an especially busy few weeks, with some of the more gargantuan acts on the planet hanging out night after night.

The Kings of Leon became fixtures at the hotel after their fourth album *Only by the Night* exploded around the world after its release in September 2008. Them Crooked Vultures had just formed and began early practice sessions in a villa directly above the bar. Hip-hop and rap stars Usher, Lil Wayne, and Eminem spent a fair amount of time with us. Ronnie Wood of the Rolling Stones ordered a shot of tequila from me one day, and I nearly died from ecstatic conniption. Tori Amos, Van Morrison, Cyndi Lauper, Carrie Underwood, Morrissey, Billy Gibbons, a plethora of exasperatingly attractive actors and actresses…okay, okay, I'll stop, I'll stop. Wait, two more. David Coverdale made his first appearance around this time, and to this day I have never met anyone like him. You may need to be a music lover like me to appreciate how incredibly iconic the bands Deep Purple and later Whitesnake were, but the man responsible for both was nothing short of, let's say, fucking awe-inspiring. As was polarizing sports idol Lawrence Taylor when we had him for two different stints during his time on *Dancing with the Stars*. But I'm not one to get starstruck, this book isn't a tell-all, and I'm a firm believer in the loyalty I'll always owe the Marquis, so we'll stop with the name-dropping right here. Besides, the celebrities didn't make up the best part of that job.

"Oh?"

Seriously. It was those five barstools and what they afforded me. Salary and tips, sure, but way more than that. The very thought of a bar summons a variety of images, but many of them are of a sad, beer-soaked tavern bathed in artificial light or a rowdy pub where drink orders are shouted to be heard over the music as sloppy patrons turn over every thirty seconds. That was not my bar.

Many of my customers would sit for hours. Most weren't celebrities or Hollywood big shots; they were hotel guests or neighborhood dwellers who liked to get out of their apartments. I got to know many of these patrons intimately. I got to converse, and soak up knowledge, and make them intricate libations or be their counselor for the night. The restaurant goers were often in larger parties of four or six or eight, and I rarely wandered into the restaurant, but the bar patrons were often alone or paired off with another person. My people skills were sharply honed during my spell there…one riveting conversation at a time. Then again, naturally, the other major part of the job was working well-funded parties. Never-ending numbers of parties.

Okay, one final name-drop.

Matthew McConaughey and crew took over the garden grove area after the restaurant had closed for the night. My manager asked me to stay on to handle the bartending duties. It was supposed to be a small affair, but it ended up four times the size expected, and my manager also had to hop behind the bar just so we could keep up. Still, the big thing that made an impression on me was what the party was for and how excited everyone was to be there, especially McConaughey himself. *Ghosts of Girlfriends Past* is a relatively unremarkable film, and at the time, maybe his fifth or sixth romantic comedy. But you would think by the sheer celebration of life that unfolded it was the first movie he ever starred in and that it was going to make bajillions at the worldwide box office. Point being, the man clearly understands that everything, big or small, is worthy of a celebration, and that all victories in life should be honored.

More to the point, this was perhaps my first real taste of what it means to "Prosper Today." My first cognizant recognition of the credo, as it were. And though I had yet to be formally introduced to the divinity, I was certainly witnessing the actions of one very tranquil Hanged Man. One who quaffed from the fountain of fame while laughing in the face of its absurdity. As if he hadn't already starred in *EdTV*, *The Wedding Planner*, *How to Lose a Guy in 10 Days*, *Sahara*, *Failure to Launch*, and *Fool's Gold*. Not to mention the abundance of critically acclaimed films in between those films. Fucking *Ghosts of Girlfriends Past*? Ha! Okay, I hear you, McConaughey. I see you and your loved ones building a bonfire to the night sky, and I appreciate the context of your luminescent aura, good sir!

When the party was over, he was somehow the last man standing as well as the one who'd have to pay for the overages of the excess consumption. My manager and I stood right next to him as he looked over the very large bar bill. He didn't flinch. Didn't bat an eye. Didn't question a thing or even twitch a facial muscle, if I recall correctly. But he didn't just sign off and pay for the bill either. He studied it first. Took the time to appraise the damages as they lay. He could have just covered the extra couple grand as easy as most of us throw some change into the tip jar at a coffee bar, but he didn't. He had caroused like a warrior of noted spirit, outlasted every soul who was earlier there to drink from his teat, and then he contemplated and ultimately paid that fucking bar tab. I learned a great deal from a lover of Buddhism that night.

Overall, life at the bar was going well, yes, but now it was time to get serious about real estate. Clearly, I really like doing a ton of shit at once, and 2009 was a classic example of my nature playing out. For starters, I aspired to get my own broker license so that I could have my own realty brokerage someday, with agents under my employ, and be a real estate investor. I got the ball rolling in the spring and officially earned my license in July. And while that was happening, I offered my services as a buyer's agent to anyone who would have me. Oh, and perhaps you're wondering what was going on with all that dysfunctional real estate in Syracuse and Missouri?

"I definitely was."

I was fielding an abhorrent number of calls from banks and credit cards and water and power departments looking to be paid, which, while distracting and painful at times, also served as another in a long line of life's lessons about what is noise and what demands immediate attention. These creditors did not demand immediate attention, nor did I end up filing for bankruptcy. I patiently waited out their threats while accruing enough money to settle with them when the time was right. For now, the time was right for me to be as big of a wiseass as I could to anyone who called me for a payment. That put a smile on my face at least once a week. Then…

It was a relatively benign Marquis party over the summer that would bring me my first repeat client. A garrulous real estate investor just happened to be at a hotel event and was busting my chops for fun, and I was doing my best to keep up with the banter. I told him a little about myself and he offered me an opportunity to write offers for his investment outfit if I followed up with him. He probably thought I'd flake, but I called the next day and found myself in his offices a few days later, meeting all his partners and impressing upon them that I would happily do all the grunt work they needed. They accepted.

The rest of the year was filled with ninety-hour workweeks and as many realty closings as I could muster. By the time my one-year hotel anniversary rolled around, I had helped a few clients buy some smaller pieces of property, I was writing tons of offers and closing a select few of them for my real estate investor client, and I was working hard to secure a solid listing as well as continuing to accrue buyers. I had even created my own realty shingle, which I could market as an extension of Keller Williams since I was a full-fledged broker now.

However, to be clear, the money I was making in realty was marginal compared to what I was pulling down at the bar, so I was nowhere close to leaving the Marquis. Not to mention I was in the throes of my education about what it would take to make it as a full-time investor. The honeymoon phase between me and the hotel may have been over, but I was still thankful to have that job and still enjoying the lifestyle and perks the Marquis afforded. Until…

Jury duty.

"Jury duty? Come on now."

Not just any fucking jury duty, good people. Somehow, I managed to get myself chosen as one of the twelve who would be deciding a first-degree murder case. The crazy thing is that during the selection process the judge asked all potential jurors if any of us had a history (or bias, as it were) that included damage of personal property. Uh, yes, the Syracuse and Saint Louis houses had seen their fair share of abuse, including that one time someone broke into one of them and left a box of chemicals on a lit stove in an attempt to blow up the joint. But did I speak up? Surely, I did not. So then I was helping decide a murder case. Excuse me, a first-degree murder case.

Allow me to paint you the scenario the judge painted for us on the first day of the trial: in the state of California, if you are a getaway driver, waiting in the car while your armed accomplice walks into a bank and points their weapon at a bank teller, and that teller drops dead of a heart attack from the shock of being robbed, you as the getaway driver are guilty of first-degree murder. No pleading and definitely no fucking ifs, ands, or buts.

It was Awards Season at the hotel again, I had realty clients and open escrows that needed attention, but I had to be in downtown Los Angeles every weekday morning by seven thirty to help decide the fate of a youth barely out of his teen years who may or may not have been the mastermind behind a neighborhood robbery gone horribly wrong.

I remember a great deal from this trial: the sadness of a grieving family who showed up in court every day looking for justice. The inescapable fact that the defendant had become entrenched with neighborhood gang activity but had not himself joined the gang. And though the gang member accomplices to the crime were defendants in their own separate trials, we as jurors were somehow supposed to take this into consideration and disregard certain facts about the other trials at the same time. The public defender was poor at their job, but the public prosecutor may very well have been worse. The judge was incredibly good at their job and was often doing the work of both defense lawyer and prosecutor when they failed to do theirs. The defendant was potentially looking at life in prison over what amounted to a few hundred dollars stolen from an oversized Coke Bottle bank and the tragic loss of life in which the defendant almost certainly did not pull the trigger or even have any inkling one was going to be pulled that fateful day. The police officers who took the stand lied. A number of times. And it became clear as day that even if you are innocent beyond all doubt for literally anything, including a routine traffic stop, you should never, ever, AND I MEAN FUCKING EVER speak to the police without a lawyer present.

This is not an indictment of police officers and the job they do, nor is it an indictment of the overarching "shield" that protects our communities. This is a witnessed judgment of the criminal justice system that proved itself woefully arcane over the course of this trial. Because when taxpayer time and money are spent prosecuting an individual, the job of the prosecutor is to convince the jury of the defendant's guilt by any means necessary, and the job of the police is to help corroborate that guilt by any means necessary.

"I knew that already."

Everyone who ever watched an episode of *Law & Order* THINKS they know this already. You really know it when you're watching the fate of a person's future play out directly in front of you.

The defendant's ultimate guilt or innocence aside, I will tell you that I voted guilty on all counts of murder, robbery, and battery because by the letter of the California penal code, the defendant was guilty, and the law is the law. But…we also deliberated for days because I fought like hell inside that jury room to convince any other juror who would listen that throwing away decades of the defendant's life in the name of embellished justice did not seem right. Likewise, that the evidence presented did not conclusively confirm his guilt of murder in the first degree beyond a reasonable doubt. Two of my fellow jurors agreed, and though we all confirmed his guilt for robbery and battery, we were a hung jury on murder.

"Bullshit!"

Not remotely one word of bullshit here, my friends. It went down exactly like that.

I do not know if the state deemed this case worthy of another trial, and I do not know what ultimately became of the defendant, but I'll never forget that our jury foreperson apologized to the judge when reading our verdicts. As if we had let down the justice system. And you might think a murder trial like that lasted months, but it took LESS than three weeks all said and done. Although, yes, it certainly felt like months. I can't speak for my fellow jurors, but it left me both bushed and dazed for quite a while. I can only imagine how the families involved in the trial must have felt.

"Holy crap."

The holiest of craps.

Springtime had been the perfect remedy for many a dreary winter previously, and this guy (me) was in dire need of some of that action in 2010. I was beyond ready to put the exhaustion of the trial and concurrent real estate workload behind me, and I was especially ready to leave the bartending life and work just one career. At least for a little while. And that's exactly what I set out to do, as fast as I could do it.

By this time, I had reached settlements on all credit card and personal loans as well as utilities in Syracuse. My real estate investment partners and I also agreed that I would remain responsible for the Syracuse properties currently in foreclosure while another one of the partners took on the Missouri deals. I never let my car payment go into default, so all I had on the books were the Syracuse mortgages, which were still a long way off from any real conversation of settlement because the banks were up to their eyes in a bottleneck of foreclosures. Mine could wait.

Hustling. Hard. Extra shifts at the hotel's front bar on weekends for more cash. I picked up another real estate investor client (at an investment club meeting) to write offers for. I was learning about short sales and how real estate investors buy up property for less than what was owed on the mortgage before it ever became a full foreclosure. I even started helping other real estate investors look for and file the paperwork on those opportunities.

My goal was to say goodbye to the bar and focus entirely on real estate by Memorial Day. Damn close! It took until the week of July 4. I worked one more great summer holiday, and a few regulars who knew I'd be moving on gave me some truly benevolent tips as a parting gift. My very last day at the hotel I ordered twenty pizzas and gave the night staff a little gift of my own as a thank-you for an incredible two-year (almost) journey.

When I was fourteen years old my father had moved us from a little town north of New York City out to Denver, Colorado, in search of a less hectic way of life. That was the summer of 1993 before my sophomore year of high school. Three years later, in 1996, I attended Indiana University in Bloomington and earned a Bachelor of Science from the Kelley School of Business. In 2000, I graduated college with a relatively shitty GPA, worked at DirecTV for a summer back in Denver, put as much cash in my pocket as possible, and then packed up my car and moved to Los Angeles in August of that same year.

I wanted to be a writer and a producer in Hollywood more than anything, and I tramped directly on that path for a few years after landing in Los Angeles. But, as is often the case, life pulls you in a slew of directions, jobs come and go, health has its say, relationships sway you this way or that, and you either adjust accordingly or get swept away with the tide. I wasn't quite ready to be swept away, so I adjusted into a service industry gig and relearned the essence of hustle. Hell, I downright devoured the essence of hustle while learning the significance of forgoing my own horseshit. Willfully leaving it with the rest of the proverbial cow patties, as it were. Purposefully seeking out truth, and only truth, in an effort to ascertain my own little slice of understanding of cosmic law and order. Undeniably working like a dog to overcome shortcuts and welcome certitude while embracing the suffering it took to source my dharma. A Buddhist hustler to my core.

In 2010, when I left that little bar behind, a decade had passed from the time I had moved to town. A decade of indignation and false starts and failing health and poor investments and wounded pride and the Great Recession. But just as assuredly, a decade of accumulating rope and sourcing a tree and preparing my vital organs for the impending inversion.

"Sorry? What's all this now?"

Hanged Man, ya milksop! Pay attention. This decade forged the first of my paradoxes, and I gained abundances of knowledge. Guzzling cognition as Odin intended. Reveling in truths the likes of which can be found in Vegas at 4:11 a.m. on a Wednesday. Cherishing small victories only a reformed addict like *Trainspotting*'s Renton could elocute so well. Downright PROSPERING TODAY, like McConaughey himself!

Hanged Man was upon me, and there was no turning back. Nor would I ever want to turn back. I spent eons from childhood to teenage years fantasizing what my life would be like when I finally got to Los Angeles. That is not overstatement. I was eight years old when *Platoon* was released in theaters, and even though there was no fucking way my parents would let me near it, I obsessed for months about my chance for a viewing. Months. Years even. I knew right then and there that I would one day move to Los Angeles and work in Hollywood. That was the only real truth I knew for most of my adolescent life. That one day, someday, I would get to live my lifelong fantasy. And though the decade-long ride from 2000 to 2010 hadn't nearly resembled that fantasy, the absolute truth was, it had been even better.

CHAPTER TWO

A PURITANICAL PAGAN

MY FIRST INTRODUCTION to the term *pagan* was in the film *Dragnet*. Tom Hanks in his early wiseass days, Dan Aykroyd at his loquacious best, and the ever-affable Christopher Plummer wholly crushing the role of Reverend Jonathan Whirley—who turns out to be the head of the Pagan Underground. In the film, P.A.G.A.N. stands for People Against Goodness And Normalcy. And one unforgettable scene (at least unforgettable to an impressionable ten-year-old who venerated any form of comedy) invoked lavish goat costumes, possessed dancing, a virgin sacrifice, a gargantuan sea serpent, and apparently all the amphetamines on the planet. Pure heretical madness. You know—*gasp*—fucking godlessness!

Of course, a pagan is simply someone who holds religious beliefs that differ from those of the world's main religions. But because pagan beliefs are often associated with Satanism or Wicca or Heathenry, being a pagan easily conjures the image of a treacherous iconoclast. The word itself is an undoubted negative, but where did it originate and why? I ask because, unlike the dissidents from the movie, in real life there was never really a subset of people who called themselves pagans. *Others* called them that, and that's an important distinction.

Others like the church.

"Excuse me?"

THE CHURCH. Better? That's who named them pagans. The Christian church. In the fourth century, during the rule of Emperor Constantine, the first emperor to convert to the faith, Christianity became the adopted religion of the Romans. And in case you didn't know, the Roman Empire was kind of a big deal on Earth at the time, so if the emperor was doing it, everybody figured they should make the jump too. And if not? Prepare to be deemed permanently inferior. Hence the very broad definition of paganism: *the religion of the peasantry.*

I am a pagan. Wait, wait, wait, wait, wait…chill. I bear no upside-down pentagram tattoos, hug no trees, and I worship no god. Zero gods. But outdated terminology can often be harmful, and, well, words do matter. For instance, is a child truly illegitimate because she was born out of wedlock? Like, honest to goodness illegitimate? Because that's the term we still use in courts of law to describe ones birthed to unwed mothers. Illegitimate. As in, *not sanctioned by law or custom.* As in, *illegal, criminal, felonious.* And if you want to keep branding children as illegitimate before they've even had a chance to open their eyes to the world for the first time, then go ahead and brandish me a pagan. I'll even wear it like a badge of honor for ya.

Hell, I am definitely a Person Against Goodness And Normalcy.

"Nihilist!"

Not quite. As you will see shortly, I believe in plenty.

"Fascist!"

Okay, now you're just shouting names at me. Let me clarify here: I am against the institutional depictions of Goodness and

Normalcy. As it stands now, one could argue that the world is run by those who believe in a higher power. It's a strong argument, I might add. Consider, there are 195 countries in the world, and a clear majority of their principal leaders either believe in God or pretend to, to maintain their rule. Christ, in 30 specific countries you MUST belong to a particular religion to be head of state.

"Blasphemer!"

Yeah, you got me on that one, I did just use the supposed Lord's name in vain to make a point. Good on you. But it's certainly not blasphemy to point out that nearly one-sixth of the realms that make up the United Nations demand their ruler be of a certain religion.

And while there are so many nations and so many heads of state and so many different religions, it seems unfair and perhaps even irresponsible to lump them together as one ideal of believer the very same way pagans have come to be lumped into one ideal of heretic. Ah, but therein lies the rub, right? I'm the irresponsible one. The terribly wicked fucking pagan atheist lumping all these different heads of state who embrace God into just one notion of "believer." How dare I?!

It may surprise you to know that I grew up an observant Jew. All right, not follow-all-six-hundred-thirteen-laws-to-a-tee observant but maybe more like eight laws observant. My family attended High Holiday services, and we celebrated (and commiserated on, in some instances) the important Jewish calendar days. Plus, I went to Hebrew school for oh so, so, so many fucking years so I could be bar mitzvahed. And, having retained most of the Hebrew alphabet, I can even still read the Torah a bit. Can't understand a word of it, but yeah, I can read the damn thing. But, like I said, I'm out on religion entirely now. Splitsville. The Big Sayonara. Secularism or bust, mofo. What can I tell you? I'm not one to mince words, so hear me loud and clear when I say this—I'm obsessive about the truth, and the truth is, there is no truth in God.

"You just had to say it, didn't you? Bastard!"

Hey, what did I just tell you about my thoughts on illegitimate children? Sheesh.

Perhaps *God* is not the right word. We (the collective biosphere) throw that term around as if it were something all seven billion plus of us can relate to. The side-splitting irony is that none of us can, since all of us might as well be saying "my" God. That's right. Every single time the holy one's name is uttered. Every prayer, every sermon, every suicide bombing, every blessed orgasm. All who believe should consider what it means to invoke God into anything, when in fact, they are invoking "their" own God.

And to drill down deeper, I am not merely speaking about how the Jewish God compares to the Christian God. I am talking about how the Christian God compares to the Christian God. Or the Islamic God compares to the Islamic God. Every single person who belongs to a faith and worships God is worshipping "their" own God. Their snowflake version of who/what/where God is in their mind. God is not the argument, because you can't ever argue with "my" God. There is no objective truth in it.

Creator is the right word. Creator is the big quarrel. All the major (along with a substantial number of minor) religions include some notion of a creator.

But there is no truth in a creator.

There, it has been said doubly. There is no one creator of the heavens and earth. There is no one creator who is constantly watching over quadrillions of stars across trillions of galaxies. And if you're a believer who wants to tell me that maybe there are multiple creators watching over multiple worlds, then you best bite your tongue because that is antithetical to any earthbound monotheistic dogma anyone currently subscribes to.

"Okay, time out. Time the eff out!"

Yes?

"Where is all this coming from?"

My mind.

"No, I mean, why are you telling me all this?"

Because *God* is humanity's greatest contradiction of all, and I find it best to get right to the heart of any matter. Especially one so personal to, well, everyone.

"And you want me to stop believing in God?"

I didn't say that. But I am absolutely saying that I want you to start believing in yourself. Now, as I was pontificating earlier: multiple creators watching over multiple worlds is antithetical to any earthbound monotheistic dogma anyone currently subscribes to.

"Okay, well, uh, what about polytheistic dogmas?"

What about them? None is concerned with worlds beyond our own in relation to spreading the gospel. I'll concede that a smattering of religions tout alien life as part of their creed (Scientology and the evil galactic overlord Xenu come to mind), but now we're way off the reservation here. Especially since we ALL couldn't for sure agree aliens have visited us and imparted their religious beliefs, which means all known religious subscription begins and ends with earthbound human beings.

What we CAN all agree on is that there are six scientific kingdoms of life: plants, animals, protists, fungi, archaebacteria, and eubacteria. And where do they all exist? Yep, earth. And how did they all get here? Time, pressure, and a delicate combination of cosmic dust and evolution, that's how. Any alternative conversation on the matter is a subscription to Creationism.

"No you did not! Did you REALLY just tell me I'm an effing Creationist?!"

If you believe in "your" God or a "Creator" of any kind, you bet I effing did.

Look, I'm an ardent supporter of free speech and practicing your religious beliefs at liberty, so please understand that this is not the overall qualm. What I am getting at is that there is no justifiable reason to fuse science and religion under any circumstances anymore. So, if you believe in God in any capacity, you are a Creationist. And if you do, and you are, then own it. Why wouldn't you? The 30 specific theocracies and 165 other countries who all almost undoubtedly feature God-fearing heads of state all do, and they run everything. Their borders alone are meant to represent Goodness and Normalcy. Regardless of continent, great societies have conspired so that land borders confirm the status of their citizenry and that "God Almighty" has sanctioned their existence.

"Uhhhh…"

Uhhhh is right.

The United States is no exception, and we should owe a great debt of gratitude for our sovereignty to the power upstairs. Golly, we might as well have a Pledge of Allegiance in our public schools that mentions God, and we should probably put a mention of God on our money, and we should absolutely make sure anyone intent on governing from the White House believes in God before we dare elect them. Yup, exactly. Again, color me pagan.

"You're one of those self-hating former zealots, aren't you?"

You think so, tough ass? Then, why do I live in a neighborhood in Los Angeles that is peppered with zealous Jews?

"Sorry, what's that again?"

It's true. The streets north, south, east, and west of my house are peopled with devout Jews. Is it a coincidence that I settled into a pocket of such religious influence from my own background? Partly yes, because I landed in my current house while working at the Sunset Marquis, which was a lifesaver at the time. Yet I've lived here for nearly ten years, and I've had ample opportunity to relocate. What keeps me here? Well, familiarity, delicious restaurants, low rent, sure, but it's more than that. Maybe it's divinity.

"Divinity, is it? This freaking guy's all over the place!"

Am I now? Or am I right where I told you I'd be from the onset? Comfortably upside-down and intoxicatingly nuzzled by the warmth of my own contradictions.

"*Harrumph!*"

Don't fret, we'll get you there soon enough. I promise.

There are two major sects of Jews: Ashkenazic and Sephardic. Sephardim hail from Spain, North Africa, and the Middle East. Ashkenazim descend from France, Germany, and Eastern Europe. I am Ashkenazi, which mostly means I have lighter skin and a worse digestive system than my Sephardic brethren.

My neighborhood Israelites are almost all Ashkenazim, like me, though that's where the similarities end. For instance, they enjoy donning wool garments from head to toe, outfits that often include fur hats in the dead heat of summer, whereas I prefer wearing comfortable clothing at all times. They eat kosher and pray multiple times a day. I eat whatever my belly allows and pray never. They schedule their time around a bountiful number of Jewish holidays and the weekend Sabbath. I schedule my time around whatever my wife and child want to do. So, okay, kind of the same thing on that one.

I also go out of my way to avoid them. Even when they try to engage me in conversation, I shun them and claim I am too busy to speak. Even when they invite me to holiday festivities or ask me to partake in high holiday traditions, I do my best to make myself unavailable. Is it guilt? Is it because I need to constantly and fervently prove that I've given up on religion now?

"See? You are self-loathing."

Maybe you're right.

"I am?"

I am human. I have doubts and sensitivities that lie beyond my control. So, sure, at times I feel the inadequacies that a self-loather might feel. But I am devout in my secularism now, which is the main justification for my avoidance of my neighbors. They represent the deepest corners of my heritage, yet they have no tolerance for even the surface corners of my newfound atheism. There is no reasoning with them. There is only the smiling face of their own devoutness and the expectation that I be part of the fold, followed by the inevitable smiling face of disappointment for taking up space in their neighborhood when they learn I will not be folding, even partly.

"I see your point."

My son did not receive a bris (the traditional Jewish ceremony of circumcision). What we did instead is our business, so I'll leave it at that. My cousin also married a non-Jewish person, they also had a son a few months after ours was born, and they too debated whether to have a bris. I passionately lobbied for them to have the bris.

"Huh? You still lobbied for that even after drawing your line in the sand?"

Sure did. Because they intend to raise their son Jewish, and a bris is a foundational imperative to start the child's Jewish journey. A bris is literally a covenant with God. What they decided to do is their business, so we'll leave it at that, too, but I hope it's becoming clearer that I'm not opposed to spirituality. What I'm opposed to is the notion that a belief in a higher power combined with an unflinching devoutness to your chosen doctrine is the only acceptable way to prove your spirituality.

For instance, whereas I unabashedly support a strong belief in yourself, I also subscribe wholeheartedly to serving something other than yourself. And, well, it is conceivable to serve a power that doesn't begin with the letter *G* and end with the letter *D*, because servitude is a construct that does not require ten commandments. Moreover, I believe willing servitude is the most altruistic of cleansers available on the market.

"What market?"

The market of "human capital," my friends. *Intangible collective resources possessed by individuals and groups within a given population.* Not all the collective resources have to be put toward economic gain. Some of those collective resources should simply warm the cockles of the heart. Like willing servitude, for example. Altogether too many terrible forms of servitude have set back human advancement, yet *willingly* serving the greater good is the embodiment of forward movement. Plus, volunteering just feels fucking awesome, doesn't it? Not to mention how paramount it is to a healthy soul. That's right, I the pagan, I the religious heretic believe in the soul. I felt mine inside of me the day my niece drowned.

"Oh, I am so sorry."

This is delicate. This is so delicate for a number of reasons, most important of which is that I am exposing personal family tragedy. Family is everything, and I would sooner snap off one of my own limbs than purposefully hurt my kin. Which means we are absolutely not getting into the particulars of the incident, and the only reason I specified how she died is to encapsulate a level of pain this comes with as opposed to, say, watching a child suffer through a fatal disease over time. They don't need comparing, so let's not, but the abruptness of the occurrence is what sticks with me. More, the timing of my telling you may come off as…calculated since I just finished railing against God's existence, and information of this nature tends to pull on a heartstring or two. Judge me as you will.

She was two when she died. I take sick days about as often as Halley's Comet appears, so the fact that I just happened to be home nursing a horrific cold when the call came is something I'll never forget. My wife (fiancée at the time) and I had just come back from New York, where we were visiting my family and where we spent a great deal of time with my niece. We boarded a flight from Los Angeles back to New York that same night.

The physical pain that began burrowing between my third and fourth ribs on that flight is what I remember most. The aching, never-ceasing, not unbearable, but undeniably numinous pain. That is where MY soul is located. The pain was there for months, and when it was gone, I missed its possession of me.

Cynics such as me will tell you the presence of pain was a manifestation of grief and psychological trauma that made me feel an ache behind my rib cage. It was my soul. Cynics such as me will tell you that when asked to imagine a soul, a vast number of people project its existence as somewhere in the trunk region, between our belly button and our lower neck. Cynics such as me can feast on plentiful amounts of beetle shit. It was my soul. The soul is immortal. It will live on long after our bodies give out. It will seep into the soil, or it will materialize into vapor, destined to diffuse into the farthest elements in the cosmos. It will do these things because consciousness does not require a vessel such as an animal physique to exist, and the soul reflects our consciousness. The "Creator" may not abound, but we sure do. So, too, do our souls.

Buddhists do not believe in a soul.

"What the...? You might literally be leading me in circles here."

Yes, of course I am. Did you think there was such a thing as closure? No, no, no, no, my friends. There is no such notion as closure. Nor should there be. We are cyclical beings and we abide in a cyclical milieu. Day into night and around into day again. The seasons in a year. Annual circuits around our sun. The once-every-billion-years rotation of all disc galaxies in the universe around the black holes at their center. And here on Earth, all six kingdoms have their own cycles. Humans especially. Physical cycles. Emotional cycles. Cycles inside of cycles. Time and space are not linear. Nothing in nature is linear. Also, what did I say right at the beginning of Chapter 1? I am not a Buddhist, nor do I subscribe to or intend to subscribe to Buddhism.

It is a religion, after all, and I'm still out on organized religion. What I am in on is the suffering. Specifically, the main takeaway of the Noble Truths of Buddhism: *All life is suffering.*

"So you've mentioned. But that sounds so morose."

Yet another wonderful contradiction, if I may say so, but fomenting despondency is not the purpose of the Noble Truths. They are meant to remind us that despite the fact that our time on earth will not be all sunshine and rainbows, what we do on our journey while we're here is what matters most. This is merely a reality of what it means to be human, and life without suffering could never begin to define the experience of life to begin with. A transformative, eternal quotation from eminent peace advocate Norman Cousins sums up this ideal and lent me strength to cope with the loss of my niece: *Death is not the greatest loss in life. The greatest loss is what dies inside us while we live.*

Another example? I agree. Something larger in scope and that will take my mind away from dwelling on what happened to my beloved niece. Spin the wheel…spin the wheel…and…how about American football? Fantastic choice!

I am a lifelong New York Jets fan. Oh, fuck, here it comes. I'll wait, go on, I just blew up your spot for a good ten pages there. By all means, make all the "suffering" jokes you need to get it out of your system.

"No title since 1969. No good quarterback since Joe Namath, and even he finished with a sub-five-hundred record. They play in the freaking swamps of New Jersey, not even New York State proper. The infamous 'Butt-Fumble.'"

Wakka wakka. Are you finished? No? A few more? Fine, go ahead, motherfucker.

"The New England Patriots owning you for nearly two decades now. The Tim Tebow trade. The endless draft busts. Bill Belichick coming to your rescue and then resigning one day into the job as your head coach."

That last one was totally uncalled for!

"Hehe."

Feel better?

"Much."

Fantastic.

The putrid stink of a floundering franchise aside, the game itself shall be our focus, not my debilitated squad. It is clear now that playing tackle football is bad for your health. More specifically, repeatedly bashing your head into another person is detrimental to the health of your brain and its surrounding protective layers. The science is in. Protect yourself as best you can with pads and helmet (and padded helmets), you're still not coming out of too much time on the field unscathed. And until we uncover even worse diseases, chronic traumatic encephalopathy, also known as CTE, is the hot-button affliction of the moment. CTE results from repetitive brain trauma, as the protein tau forms clumps that spread throughout the brain, killing brain cells as it does. And though it is currently inconclusive whether every single NFL player will contract CTE, a 2017 study from Boston University researchers found signs of CTE in 177 out of 202 brains of those who had ever played organized football, including 110 out of 111 brains of deceased NFL retirees.

Here is a short list of the symptoms of CTE:

- Impulsive behavior
- Depression
- Emotional instability
- Substance abuse
- Suicidal thoughts

The evidence that CTE will trouble legions of NFL retirees in the latter part of their lives is mounting quickly, and the profiles of some of the game's most vaunted stars are stockpiling annually now. Junior Seau was a prolific defensive player who shot himself in the chest, killing himself and mimicking another prolific defender, Dave Duerson, who also shot himself in the chest a year earlier. Seau left no suicide note, but Duerson did, which specifically requested that his brain be studied for effects of trauma. Frank Gifford, Ken Stabler, and Bubba Smith are three of the biggest names to have been confirmed afflicted with CTE. And then there is Aaron Hernandez. His bright career was cut short when he was arrested for murder, for which he was later found guilty, and for more than one murder, and sentenced to life in prison. He hanged himself in his cell in 2017. The Boston University study made specific note of Hernandez, claiming his CTE was the most severe they had ever seen for someone his age. He was twenty-eight at the time of his death.

Again, the above-mentioned men are all deceased. It was only in November 2017 that researchers believed they detected CTE in the first living NFL retiree. It will take many years to perfect testing to unequivocally prove CTE in living persons and—even more detrimental to football at every level, from Pee Wee to the NFL—in current players. But between now and then? I'm unquestionably going to watch pro football and root for my shitty team.

Some part of me wishes that weren't true. Some part of me wants to sign petitions or just turn off the fucking television in solidarity to help save these men's lives. But that's the elitist prig talking, not the beast who craves his weekly dose of perpetual war. I am that beast. The brutality is intoxicating. Feed me bone-jarring hits along the sidelines. Deliver me platters of your finest smackdowns over the middle of the field. Satisfy the beast's craving for the glorious sound of a helmet crashing into another helmet. Like fucking *thunder*, I tell you! Injury timeouts be damned. The cart gracing the field for a more serious injury be double-damned. Prayer circles for the immobilized player taken away by stretcher be gone. The beast wants perfectly executed end arounds and flea-flickers and jaw-dropping punt returns and blindside sacks and trips right and guards checking in as receivers and cornerback blitzes and both feet inbounds and Hail Marys at the end of the first half and QBR graphics and cartoonish arguing with referees and one-handed catches and impish touchdown celebrations. The beast doesn't want to hear from ruptured Achilles tendons or neck stingers or dislocated fingers or broken clavicles or herniated discs or chronic traumatic encephalopathy, for fuck's sake. The beast has no interest in the suffering, pain, and misery it takes to put points on the board—all the beast wants is for his team to put more points on the board than the other fucking team!

My son will never play tackle football on our watch. This does not mean we intend to hide him away from physical altercation. In fact, I hope he finds his way into wrestling because there are few better sports to teach numerous life lessons. Lacrosse can be brutal, but he can certainly play if he so chooses. Soccer is notorious for concussions. Have at it, kid. Martial arts I'm all good with. Boxing? I'd rather he didn't, but if something inside of him yearns to know if he can take a punch (or many), I'd make my peace with it. But football is a never. Not while my wife and I agree and while we still get to be the ones signing the permission slips.

"A lot of people are starting to feel this way."

Uh-huh, every once in a while, I get to preach to the choir.

But I take no joy in this discourse. I mean to give no sermon about the ultimate dangers of football. I really don't. I would much rather football keep succeeding. To some who see no appeal in football to begin with, this is a moot point. Others are finding reasons beyond CTE to leave the game behind, including (but not limited to) a dilution of product. Dilution from an imperfect league schedule that exhausts players and dilution from too many rule changes that take away from the violence many of us have come to expect to see. Then there is the social unrest, with players protesting racial injustices by kneeling during the national anthem and advocates of the military turning that into an assault on the armed forces. And finally, the wildly misconstrued belief by team owners and their lackey commissioner that the NFL logo has come to represent Lady Liberty and all her freedoms and that it is their ironic duty to snipe out threats to the shield by ruling over their dominion with an iron fist. Still, all those distractions pale in comparison to the havoc that CTE and other maladies will ultimately wreak upon the league. This is what I mean by suffering.

It took decades for American football to find its footing and its audience, but by the mid-1970s it was firmly woven into the national consciousness. And if you enjoy sports even a little, football represents the apex of why you might. All sports have their rules, and then finely tuned athletes compete to bend those rules to their will. All while we get to watch in awe.

"With a ton of camera angles, no less."

That's what I'm talking about!

Football specifically inspires that feeling of awe at an incredible rate, right? Then there are the nuances of the game. Some might be bored to see a two-yard run up the middle, but true fans appreciate the scheming it took from all twenty-two players on the field just to eke out those two yards on that one play. Then that play is followed by another play. Followed by another. All with endless combinations and endless results. And the clock, oh the ticking clock! Sixty minutes of calculations and terrific violence. Lest we forget about the beautiful fucking violence!

"Sure. Violence. Yeah. Although how exactly do you reconcile associating the most peaceful religion on earth with the most violent of sports?"

Because Buddhism isn't peaceful at all. It's quite vehement, with its fair share of fanaticism and self-inflicted violence, merely echoing the storm that brews inside all of humanity. Certainly inside of me. But false perception is its own kind of monster, and this really isn't about the religion as a whole. Or football for that matter. It's about Noble Truths. It's about suffering.

Decades of cultivation, masses of fanbases, millions of children. Middle schools, high schools, and colleges. Communities and local businesses. Billions of taxpayer dollars committed to stadiums. An expanding presence internationally. Merchandise that bonds enthusiasts with others across the land, and around the globe, for that matter. For all its warts—plenty of societal outlets have warts—for all its chauvinism, for all its God-thumping, chest-beating, steroid-taking narcissism, football offers an array of positive features to like as well. And, really, at the end of the day, it's a game, and humanity thrives on games. Games are an integral part of society, football is one of the more magnificent games, and football is going to be gone.

Count on it. I won't prognosticate as to when, but it won't survive. At least not in its current iteration it won't. The violence is truly hurting people—way more than season-ending injuries, we're talking about life-altering disorders. The players themselves, obviously, and their families too: spouses, children, siblings, and even parents of players. The same innovation gene that drives us to make everything bigger, faster, and stronger has reached a critical mass where mammoth bodies bash into each other with disastrous results. And it won't matter that men and women might willingly sacrifice their long-term health for short-lived glory. We're not talking about the right to use tobacco at your own discretion (an industry that has seen its own precipitous decline in customers). We're talking about a behemoth sport that is consumed by a huge portion of the population and that needs television viewers and streaming outlets to consume the content. This will ironically also contribute to the game's downfall.

"How's that exactly?"

The NFL's current broadcast dominance and exposure to the masses will one day be its biggest foible. Football will have to go local again because the powers that be will inevitably succumb to the pressure of those who demand it no longer be transmitted nationally, which comes across as tacit endorsement of the sport. Again, we're talking about a substitute for the days of gladiator games that has turned out to be as disastrously dangerous as well.

The game can't abide. The lawsuits won't abide. The generations coming who will not be allowed to participate refuse to abide. And the collective conscience of the crowd will someday overrule the outliers who fight to keep football a mainstay tradition.

"Shiiiiit. But players get hurt on the field all the time. Sometimes hurt terribly."

Which is all part of the game and the experience now, yes, so that we are sadly desensitized. But what happens when the lights turn off? Altogether too many seemingly healthy players go home to their families and suffer gravely. And then the players grow older and morbidities flourish well before they should be flourishing. Horrendous morbidities like CTE.

"But isn't that their choice? Don't the players get to decide to make that sacrifice for fame?"

Damn right they do! But—and this is a pretty big BUT here—they won't be the ones deciding who's left to watch their self-immolation.

"Shiiiiiiit."

Tell me about it.

Lavish costumes (garish uniforms), possessed dancing (balletic athletic moves), virgin sacrifice (waves of fresh players eager to give their bodies over to the cause), a gargantuan sea serpent (distracting entertainment every NFL stadium deploys to roil the crowd), and apparently all the amphetamines on the planet (all the performance-enhancing drugs one can consume). Kickoff right on time every wintry Sunday afternoon, baby. God's day. Pure heretical madness.

You know something? Regardless of what happens to the future of American football, I for one will be grateful we ever had the opportunity to enjoy such a celebrated pastime to begin with. Go, Pagans! *Whoops*. Total slip of the tongue there. Go, Jets!

CHAPTER THREE
A LIBERAL LANDLORD

For the most part, the real estate investors and private lenders I have worked with would have to be categorized as members of the GOP. Otherwise known as Grand Old Party. Otherwise known as Republican. You attend enough real estate events, you work on enough real estate ventures, you broker enough private loans, you speak to enough fellow landlords—you get an overall vibe for a certain political leaning. Me? I'm a staunch liberal.

I should clarify that. I am emphatically liberal on social issues. Because if you were to research my voting affiliation in the state of California, it would say Independent. I do not, will not, and want not to be a registered Democrat. I am absolutely not a Democrat, but I'm sure as shit not a Republican either. Yet to look at me from a strictly surface viewpoint and follow some outdated notions of what it is to be a conservative, you'd probably peg me as having a kinship with the Grand Old Party. I'm a white male, after all, forty, married, have a kid, college educated, like (love) to talk about money, and some might describe my hairstyle as "the Mitt Romney." But, no, my conscience has me leaning left. Very left.

As if the last chapter wasn't a big enough clue as to where my political affiliations lie, here's a few more to really bring it home: Religion? We can check that conversation off the list. Abortion? One hundred percent right to choose. Planned Parenthood? As many as possible in as many states as possible. Global warming? It's happening and we're responsible. Health care? Single-payer system for life, already. Immigration? The fact that we lock up even one person for an indefinite time, let alone thousands, then strip them of their alienable rights, essentially relegating them to second-class citizens on earth, should make us the criminals, not them. (This includes what we're doing at Guantanamo Bay, regardless of how dangerous even one of the detainees is.) Gay marriage? First of all, the term *gay marriage* ain't cutting it. Can we all agree that "marriage equality" has a much less condescending ring to it? And telling someone they can't do something that you can in the eyes of the law is the lowest of the low. Disgusting to the *n*th degree. It turns my stomach foul.

And yet, there are two hot-button issues you might be surprised to find me straddling the fence on. The first is gun control.

"Are. You. Freaking. Kidding. Me?!"

Kind of expected that reaction. Hear me out.

I don't own a gun, I don't plan on owning a gun, and I'd really like to get through my own life without ever bearing the responsibility of snuffing out the life of another. I find the disingenuous literal interpretation of the Second Amendment (abused by too many wannabe "regulated militia-people") as beyond oleaginous. The AR-15 assault rifle has zero business being sold on the open market, in major sporting goods chains, or to anyone under 185 years old. That goes for any weaponry employing the terms "automatic" or "semiautomatic" in their description, for that matter. The NRA? The NRA was founded in 1871 for the *primary pur-*

pose of promoting and encouraging rifle shooting on a scientific basis. Hmm. In 1934, the NRA supported the National Firearms Act, a piece of legislation intent on regulating *gangster weapons such as machine guns and sound suppressors.* Double hmm. In 1968, the NRA supported the part of the Gun Control Act that forbade the sale of firearms to convicted criminals and persons with mental illness. A fucktillion times hmm.

"Wait, go back a minute."

Talk to me.

"Why did the federal government feel we even needed something called the Gun Control Act in 1968?"

Glad you asked. The Black Panther Party was formed in Oakland, California, in 1966 as a response to police brutality. Its main purpose was to monitor the behavior of the Oakland Police Department and let them know they were being watched by their community, which Black Panther members succeeded in doing by utilizing open-carry gun laws. Policing the police, as it were. Open-carry gun laws lead us back to the Second Amendment and the "right to bear arms"; those arms are borne openly, as in, not concealed. This is a state-by-state issue, with each state mandating the law by use of licenses. Back to Oakland…

Unsurprisingly, pissed off about being watched by an openly armed revolutionary organization, the Oakland Police Department pushed for and the California legislature brought about the Mulford Act of 1967. This was legislation aimed at disallowing the carrying of loaded firearms of any kind in public. Ronald Reagan was governor of California at the time and said this about the importance of the Mulford Act: "There's no reason why on the street today a citizen should be carrying loaded weapons." He also said guns "were a ridiculous way to solve problems that have to be solved among people of good will."

"Reagan was a card-carrying member of the NRA though, right?"

Is a frog's ass watertight? In fairness, nine presidents have been NRA members, although George H. W. Bush resigned his membership in 1995 over comments executive vice president of the NRA Wayne LaPierre made in the wake of the Oklahoma City bombing.

May 2, 1967. The California Statehouse. The California State Assembly Committee on Criminal Procedure was set to meet to discuss the Mulford Act, only to be interrupted by nearly thirty members of the Black Panther Party who stormed the statehouse, loaded weapons in hand! Five members were arrested and later pled guilty to misdemeanor charges of disrupting a legislative session. Nothing about the guns. But the country started paying attention because this was the first major national media consideration the party had received.

"So, this was why the Gun Control Act of 1968 came about?"

No, not exactly. The Gun Control Act was really brought forth in 1963 after President John F. Kennedy was killed by a rifle purchased from a mail-order advertisement in the NRA magazine *American Rifleman*. (It should be noted that while this bill was being debated after Kennedy's death, the executive vice president of the NRA Franklin Orth had this to say: "We do not think that any sane American, who calls himself an American, can object to placing into this bill the instrument that killed the President of the United Sates.") The main purpose of the bill was to regulate the interstate shipment of firearms, but it languished in Congress for nearly five years until three very significant events happened in 1968:

1. Martin Luther King Jr. was shot and killed.
2. Robert F. Kennedy was shot and killed.
3. The Black Panther Party fanned flames of national fear of an armed uprising.

The bill passed in 1968, but other factions in the country besides the Black Panther Party took great umbrage with the verbiage in the bill. Namely, rural white conservatives. Meet Harlon Carter: Emory Law School graduate, one-time director of the southwestern region of the Immigration and Naturalization Service, and card-carrying member of the NRA. From its inception in 1871 all the way up until 1975, the National Rifle Association targeted mostly hunters and sportsmen as an audience, rarely getting involved in politics. But in 1975 Harlon Carter was installed as director of the Institute for Legislative Action, the NRA's new political lobbying arm he had helped create. And in 1977, at its annual convention, the benign topics of relocating headquarters to Colorado and building a recreational facility in New Mexico were set to be the main topics of discussion. What happened instead came to be known as "the Revolt at Cincinnati," where activists led by Carter took over the convention and forced an all-night voting session to replace leadership. Guess who won? Did I forget to mention that nearly fifty years earlier Carter had been convicted of murder without malice of a fifteen-year-old in Laredo, Texas, only to have that conviction overturned by the Texas Court of Appeals, which found that the judge had issued incorrect jury instructions regarding self-defense laws? I did forget to mention that?

"You're making all of this up."

I wish I were that inventive. And I won't take credit for stumbling upon all of this myself either. For a way more in-depth reporting, have yourself a listen to *Radiolab Presents: More Perfect - The Gun Show*. And if you do, though you're going to hear over an hour tilted toward liberalism (with an underlying message that guns are bad), I still maintain that gun control has its limits and we'd best be careful about vilifying those who assert their rights to own and carry a gun.

"You're talking about the military."

I am not. And that is an entirely different issue in which the public is disturbingly unaware of how gruesome gun-related military casualties are.

"You want to arm teachers in public schools."

Better, I want to give six-month vacations to members of the U.S. Capitol Police and the Secret Service, and then arm 20 percent of the legislative, judicial, and executive branches of our government and see what happens. I mean…arming teachers. Arming teachers! Fucking hell I do not want to arm teachers. Not one hallowed educator.

"What is it then? Why are you an advocate for certain gun rights?"

Because the past tells me I should be. Call me a romantic, but I get a little emotional about the revolutionary uprising that led to 1776. Hell, I get a little emotional about all revolutionary uprisings that turn out to be on the right side of history: 464 BCE: The Helot slaves revolting against Spartan masters. 40 CE: The Tru'ng Sisters uprising to free Vietnam from Chinese rule. 982 CE: The pagan Polabian Slavs revolt against the Holy Roman Empire. The first Prussian Uprising, the Mamluks, Jacquerie, Kett's Rebellion, the Second Brotherhood, Harpers Ferry, the Underground Railroad, the French Revolution, the Haitian Revolution, the 1960s counterculture sexual revolution, the Arab Spring. You get the idea.

Lest we ever forget, this nation was founded by persecuted pilgrims who got the fuck out of England, grew in number, and forged themselves into frontiers people. And despite atrocities worthy of never-ending admonishment that were inflicted upon Native Americans, the cold fact remains that lands were taken, and thirteen colonies were established up and down the Eastern Seaboard. English rule grew tiresome, declarations of independence were signed, and muskets were loaded. And when it was over, and before we fought ourselves years later only to reinvent as united again, we explored westward. We explored and we hunted and we settled the Plains, throughout the Panhandle, and across the Rockies. And that shit took grit, courage, and a fair amount of poorly distilled booze. But with all that hunting and frontier settling going on, it also took stockpiling a fair amount of armaments.

I may be a coastal progressive who likes colorful socks and stupidly expensive artisanal coffees, but I'll never begrudge my fellow Americans who don't and feel more comfortable with a pistol somewhere on their person. You can shout all the statistics and ideals you want at me: school shootings, workplace shootings, public event shootings, an outrageous number of gun accidents at home, possession of artillery by those who are mentally disturbed, gang violence, abuse of the police badge, glorification of war and gun use in video games and movies, 3D gun printing, incredibly advanced weaponry, the militarization of local law enforcement, NRA lobbyists—this is not the conversation. Don't get me wrong, each one of those issues demands attention and action, but they are often treated as one problem. A gun problem. They are not exclusively a gun problem; they are societal problems.

Despite numerous expert suggestions that should your home ever be invaded, you would be much better off escaping as fast as you can without ever engaging the perpetrator, I support your right to defend yourself with a permitted gun if you so choose. Despite the evidence suggesting the chances of you ever being involved in a localized terrorist attack are infinitesimally small, I support your right to fantasize about and maybe even spoil such an attack with your permitted gun if you so choose. And despite the fact that 2018 set a record for packaged meat consumption in the United States and that lab-grown meat is on its way (and hopefully delicious), I support your right to hunt with a permitted gun if you so choose.

Duh-huh, I know these are coming across as snobbishly backhanded support of your right to own a gun, but I really am serious about the romanticized element of revolutionary history. Specifically, American history. The backbone of this nation still comprises plenty of honorable men and women who identify themselves as hunters and riflemen and protectors of the realm.

And I really, truly, enthusiastically support that. If they want their slice of land, a cold brew, a permitted pistol/rifle/shotgun/nonautomatic gun by their bedside, and to be left the fuck alone, then respect their rights as law-abiding citizens and leave them the fuck alone. Because if there is ever a large enough revolution on our soil where lives are at stake (don't think it can't happen), I for one feel safer with just the idea of armed patriots outside of the military who are primed to either join or thwart that revolution to defend this land. And please notice I said JUST THE IDEA OF ARMED PATRIOTS because it's tyranny I fear most of all.

Tyranny is the end of the road. And though the sad truth may be that most gun owners inadvertently support authoritarian law, THEY don't often know that about themselves. Let's hope potential authoritarians don't know that either. Fucking hell yes, I understand this is a little like the canary employing a dangerous dog to keep the cat in check (or world superpowers amassing nuclear stockpiles to keep peace if you prefer), but guess what? The world is full of all types of weapons, and they aren't going away anytime soon. Neither is tyranny. Something must always keep tyranny in check. Never tyranny. Never.

The second issue I am on the fence about? Entitlements.

"That's a broad word."

Yeah, well, it's a broad political spectrum, despite what the leaders of our two major parties would have us believe. Democrats are most often associated with these programs, or handouts, or safety nets, or whatever term you prefer. They are funded by the federal government, and the most noteworthy are Medicare, Medicaid, Social Security, Unemployment, and Welfare.

"So, you are against helping people who can't help themselves?"

Oh, if only it were that simple. We're going to get to all of this, but we need to back up an instant and touch on something I glossed over rather quickly in the first paragraph of this chapter.

Raise your hand if you know what a private lender is. Even if you don't, you probably could guess, because it's exactly what it sounds like. Just as banks do, private individuals lend their money in exchange for fees and an agreed-upon interest rate. Each type of lender, banks and private lenders, must follow a different set of rules (which we don't have to get into), which leads to the fact that most private lenders lend their money only to real estate investors. Also, most private lenders truly prefer shorter-term loans than banks give out, and these "bridge loans" are best suited to the needs of real estate investors, their main pool of borrowers. Besides real estate investing myself, my main career choice since leaving the Sunset Marquis has been brokering these bridge loans between private lenders and other real estate investors.

You may recall from an earlier tirade how disenchanted I was with subprime lending and lending in general.

"I do."

Well, shit, that was before I ever learned about private lending, sometimes referred to as "hard money." Get your mind out of the gutter—nothing lascivious here, I assure you. The term derives from way back in the 1950s when the credit industry underwent massive changes and "last resort" loans for property owners became more prevalent. The "hard" moniker simply reflects the opposite of "soft" money. Soft money can be had with lower interest rates, lower fees, and longer durations. So, obviously, hard money comes with higher interest rates, higher fees, and shorter durations.

"So why the hell would anyone want one of these hard money loans?"

Ah, now we're getting somewhere.

I am, at this very moment, resisting a profusion of urges. Following any one of these urges could lead us too far into the weeds and I'd risk losing you altogether. So, I am assiduously resisting each of these urges. I am resisting the urge to superciliously preach about the standard bearer thirty-year mortgage product and its ills. I am resisting the urge to howl contemptuously about the current misconceptions about homeownership. I am resisting every urge I have to bellow plumes of disapproval of this country's centralized banking system, Fannie Mae, Freddie Mac, and a number of distorted government-assisted loan programs that don't need to be named here. I am resisting all these urges for you, dear friends, so I hope you appreciate my willpower.

"Don't hold back now on account of me."

Can't say I didn't warn you. Back to your initial question.

A hard money loan is simply a tool with financial leverage that real estate investors use to make more investments. That's it. Nothing more, nothing less. A tool. Those government-assisted loan programs I mentioned are not tools, nor should they be touted as such, because they should exist only to improve the lives of citizens who want a roof over the heads of their family. Except, unsurprisingly, they are politicized by each incoming administration, and they are manipulated to satisfy whatever statistic needs to look favorable (or unfavorable) at a given time, depending on who currently holds public office. They are expanded and contracted by legislators, and, worst of all, they farcically hinder capitalism. This is also my beef with entitlement programs. Wonderful intentions with bad execution sadly hurt capitalism.

"But capitalism clearly sucks anyway."

Wha? Wh—y? Wh—o? How cou—ld you sa—y that?

"Are you okay?"

No, I am not at all okay. I am fuckall out of breath with concern over your statement!

"But capitalism does suck."

Are you trying to give me an aneurysm?!

"Okay, okay. Calm down. Have a glass of water. Breathe."

[Breathing]. [Still breathing]! Okay, better. Pay close attention right now.

When I brokered subprime loans, my borrowers rarely had any idea what mortgage product they were agreeing to, just as I had a poor idea of what I was selling. And despite what sleek advertisements of major banks would have you believe, I feel the same way about most conventional mortgage products and the unsuspecting loan officers who sling them. Yet I have very few (basically no) conversations with real estate investors who are confused about the bridge loan they are borrowing. It is abundantly clear that they are playing the role of opportunist and that the lender is funding their endeavor for a brief period. The borrower is paying a higher premium for the opportunity, and the lender is taking a larger risk on this type of borrower and their real estate investment or subsequent business venture. The symbiosis of borrower and lender of these loans alone gives me the warm of fuzzies. The same cannot be said of entitlements. They give me *gas* and *agita.*

Sure, at their best, they are a great safety net for our citizens, and if administered cautiously, fair wealth distribution to those most in need. At their worst, they are economic drains abused by an addicted populace and manipulated by career officeholders. And though many of them, such as Medicaid, Pell grants, Emergency Food and Shelter, and Community Block Grants (just to name a few), are obviously wonderful in theory, they are ALL a constant reminder that we are a nation with one centralized bank. Oh, that pesky, no good, rotten Federal Reserve…how you exasperate the fuck out of me! Getting dangerously close to those weeds again—so gonna keep this simple. Promise. The Federal Reserve has three main functions:

1. Influencing monetary policy to achieve maximum employment
2. Regulating all other banking operations to ensure the safety of the financial system
3. *Operating and overseeing the nation's payments systems*

"Well, that all sounds pretty nice."

Does it? 'Cause it is essentially socialism.

"Yeah. See? Even our central banking system knows pure capitalism is not possible."

Can you define socialism for me, please?

"Well, no, not off the top of my head I can't. Can you?"

Any economic or political system based on government ownership and control of important businesses and methods of production.

Here's another: *A theory or system of social organization that advocates the vesting of the ownership and control of the means of production and distribution, of capital, land, etc., in the community as a whole.*

Control the money, control the markets, control the payments. Check, check, and fucking check for the Federal Reserve. Three for three. Batting a thousand percent. And, yes, I concede that there must be some form of procedure for overseeing the nation's payments (collection of monies, currency distribution, payment processing, etc.).

But influencing monetary policy to achieve maximum employment? Regulating ALL other banking operations to ensure the safety of the financial system? That's a whole lotta power for one centralized federation set up as twelve supposedly private corporations.

A federation, I might add, that after decades of policy mandating fluctuation to protect against inflation, then decided not to raise the federal funds rate (an indirect influence of short-term interest rates that affect home, auto, and credit card loans) once between 2008 and 2015, kicking a very volatile can of said inflation way down the road. A federation whose chairman eagerly endorsed the conservatorship (the Federal Housing Finance Agency took legal authority) of Fannie Mae and Freddie Mac when the shit hit the fan in 2008. A conservatorship that still exists as of this writing. A federation that committed trillions of dollars toward rescuing our financial system from its self-inflicted wounds during the Great Recession, and that oversaw the distribution of the largest bailout package in U.S. history to save some of the biggest banking giants and automobile manufacturers and insurance behemoths from their own fuckups.

And yeah, maybe it's a little glib to shine much-needed light on its questionable maneuvers while also peddling the oft-debated centralized banking model itself and passing it off as some great Hanged Man enlightenment, but please understand why I am doing so. Because Hanged Man is always in search of brutal truth, and the truth on this one is that the day we created the Federal Reserve (December 23, 1913), we convinced ourselves we had a more flexible and stable monetary system. Sure we did, Woodrow Wilson. Sure we did.

"*Gulp*. Dammit. Maybe define capitalism for me now?"

An economic system in which investment in and ownership of the means of production, distribution, and exchange of wealth is made and maintained chiefly by private individuals or corporations, especially as contrasted to cooperatively or state-owned means of wealth.

"Got it. But I still don't understand why this is so important to you."

Fair enough. Socialism and communism share one very common thread. One singular conviction that is an absolute nonstarter. As famed historian and journalist Adam Michnik once impressed upon stalwart contrarian Christopher Hitchens (ergo upon me)—when the bells and whistles of propaganda are stripped away, what is left is true clarity, an understanding that any government that operates under socialism or communism is dictating *that their citizens are properties of the state*. This is simply untenable for all time that ever was or ever will be.

"That's…a pretty good reason it's important."

Capitalism is not a perfect system, but it is a system that NEVER asks its citizens to be property of anything but themselves. The twisted maelstrom of enacting our capitalist ideals has decidedly failed, yes, but as we're about to explore, that is not a failure of capitalism, that is a failure of the current United States of America. It is also why I am resisting a bevy of urges to lead us too far into the weeds, as stated earlier. Not because we can't handle it together, but because laboriously debating fiscal culpability is best left to the bubbleheads that populate our television screens. The so-called experts are more than welcome to argue their far too narrow conversations of economics all they like—what we're interested in is the critical thought it takes to Prosper Today so that we may Perpetuate Tomorrow. And we're off to a real nice start here.

Moving on to insurance agencies. Insurance companies are supposed to safeguard us, right? Then why are they spending tens of millions in advertising dollars on an arms race to save you hundreds of dollars a year by switching among them? Try watching a popular network television show or sporting event without being bombarded by Geico, Progressive, Farmers, All State, Nationwide, State Farm, or AFLAC ads. Also, did I say "tens of millions"? More like hundreds of millions is spent on television advertising budgets. Wait, fuck that, Geico spends over a BILLION DOLLARS annually to remind you *fifteen minutes could save you 15 percent.* Never mind applying such colossal sums to lowering premiums or deductibles for consumers…just keep convincing them that saving hundreds of dollars a year on insurance is going to change their lives. Hundreds. Of. Dollars.

"Wait, aren't their competitive price wars a benchmark of capitalism?"

Are they? And great use of the word *benchmark,* by the way.

"Thanks."

Unfortunately, no, they are no such benchmarks, and we are once again being led astray.

Let's get me saying this on record—government is NOT evil. Logically, utilized correctly, government is paramount to a public's well-being. From the local to the federal level, government is an important maintainer of infrastructure and enforcer of laws. And you may have noticed something else I snuck into the beginning of this chapter that's probably going to have you scratching your head again: SINGLE-PAYER SYSTEM FOR LIFE.

"Oh yeah, you did say that! Isn't that socialist as all hell?"

It is logical welfare is what it is. It's what the government gets to provide the citizenry when the capitalist system is firing on all cylinders. GETS TO provide its citizenry, meaning certain welfares by our government are actually the desired result of capitalism. As stated in the Preamble to our Constitution, federal government is here to *establish justice, ensure domestic tranquility, provide for the common defense, promote the general welfare, and secure the blessings of liberty to ourselves and our posterity*. That sure as shit sounds like we can expect our health, comfort, and protection to be looked after by those who collect our taxes. Because, lest we keep forgetting, those doing the tax collecting work for us. Private individuals own the land in this beautiful democracy, and the elected officials are under our employ.

"It does seem kind of easy to forget that these days."

Yah, let's be a little harder on ourselves on that one, shall we?

What I am ultimately getting at here, what I want to make abundantly clear about why I am condensing all these thought avenues into sanctioning certain assistances while professing immense disdain for our current form of entitlements, is this: the money is backward.

Like it or not, money is the cartouche, graticule, and rectification on our all-encompassing world map. Money is the great equalizer. Not long after Woodrow Wilson's era, Calvin Coolidge became president and he presciently said: "The business of America is business." Preach on, Calvin! Except it's all been corrupted. It's been heisted and twisted into an unrecognizable political vortex of duplicity from both sides of the aisle. It's been misappropriated through decades of bureaucratic malfeasance from both the Left and the Right. And now? Now the money is ass-backward.

Privatized insurance, privatized prisons, privatized military, privatized water access, privatized transportation systems, and privatized data collection come to mind first. Our health and personal privacies have officially been corrupted by privatization. On the flip side, we've had a hundred-year run of a central bank dictating alarming monetary policies, overseeing ever-burgeoning national debts and deficits, and allowing for the politicization of entitlement programs and consumer protection agencies.

"But if you love private lending so much, why is all this other privatization so bad?"

Because private lending is a supplementary method of obtaining financing for real estate investors in addition to more conventional routes like, say, bank financing. Private lending isn't meant to replace savings and loan institutions or credit unions entirely.

Can we say the same about the privatization of the military, prisons, and transportation? In August 2017, there were 9,800 U.S. troops still in Afghanistan. There were also 26,000 privatized military contractors there at the same time. In 2016, state and federal prisons operated by private contractors accounted for 8.5 percent of all prisons, a 47 percent increase since the year 2000. As if even having 0.00001 percent of for-profit prisons making decisions about the lives of those incarcerated is at all okay. The same goes for transportation. And, no, I'm not talking about Uber or the impending Hyperloop; I'm talking about any privatization of public transit: buses, trains, subways, and the like. Private enterprise is the backbone of capitalism. Privatized enterprise has just become a fucked-up way to offload overwhelming government responsibilities.

"This is…oddly all very rational."

Thank you for noticing.

"How about the flip side? You snuck consumer protection agencies in there too."

Ah yes, consumer protection agencies. Don't even get me started.

"No, please, get started!"

Okay, since you asked nicely.

First, do you know how many national security agencies there are? Seventeen. I mention this because five or six would do the trick of keeping us safe and spying on us all the time just fine. The same goes for consumer protection agencies. Obviously, consumers need protection, but protection from whom exactly?

"The One Percent, of course! They're the bad guys. They've been preying on all of us and they're the reason we need consumer protection agencies in the first place! Aren't they?"

Here comes another Big. Buddhist. Sigh.

We have such an unnatural infatuation with the One Percent it would be funny if it weren't also hazardous to our mental stability. We worship their fortunes while decrying how they were amassed. We speak of their powers as if they are untouchable, yet we constantly seek to corral them into a version we can somehow possess all to ourselves. They are concurrently the bogeyman, the savior, the antichrist, and the divine to us. But more than anything, they are so inconsequential it is ridiculous that we even have a name for them at all.

Back to those agencies for a moment: it simply does not matter how many consumer protection agencies we have or what they intend to protect. The bad guys are always going to figure out a way to be bad, regardless of who is or isn't watching them, because that's who they are. But to somehow attribute much of this bad behavior to the One Percent, or those who seek to one day become or even serve at the pleasure of the One Percent, is misguided.

Do you know what we should really do with the One Percent? Much like the permitted gun holder with their cold brew and slice of land, we should leave them the fuck alone. The One Percent truly mean nothing. They are just as their name suggests, 1 percent of the population. And despite being perversely and erroneously blamed for our ever-expanding countrywide wealth gap, they are so far from the real problem that it's time we refocus. Immediately.

I am a landlord. I own rental properties. Yes, we sort of covered this in Chapter 1, but thankfully I don't own those defunct properties anymore. I own new properties, much closer to where I reside, which are much easier to maintain (though I will disclose here that I am selling them at the time of this writing). And besides rehabbing and then reselling the occasional single-family home, I also recently became enamored with syndicated multi-family opportunities. These three types of participation cover my main real estate investment activities.

I often think about my tenants. Sure, there is the usual hoping rent is paid on time each month, followed by the occasional moping when I must spend money on a repair. But I often think about their general overall tenancy compared to my general overall landlordism. I think about their families, and their jobs, and how I am privy to a horde of their personal information while they are privy to none of mine. I think about the duration of their leases and the inevitable rent increases over time. I think about insurances and protections (theirs and mine) and hidden costs that could arise. Pipes, roofs, trees, wiring, windows, ventilation, detectors. The liabilities are endless, the maintenance never-ending. And I certainly think about how all of them have expressed a desire to own their own home one day, and that the tenancies often start out with this conception. It's been expressed to me in no uncertain terms more than once that this relationship won't last long because they'll be buying their own home soon enough. That hasn't happened yet. Not once.

What's even more interesting to me is that not one tenant has ever asked me what it would take to become a homeowner. Wouldn't I be a good resource? Yes, I know Google is also a good resource, but it's hardly a replacement for speaking with someone who has actually been through the process of applications and credit runs and verifications of jobs, finances, and debt-to-income ratios, even if they didn't know I work in the lending world. I mean, I have at least some cordial relationship with each of my tenants, so picking my brain for five minutes about this isn't entirely out of the question. But then I remind myself—asking for help is hard. So is seeking to learn more from anyone for any reason. These are both understandably hard things to do.

"What's so good about being an owner of investment property anyway?"

You mean besides the cash flow, tax deduction of mortgage interest, appreciation of equity over time, and the years of depreciation you're afforded on investment property, residential and commercial alike? Let's go with the taxing of passive income in relation to the taxing of working income.

"Do tell."

Oh, you bet your ass I'm gonna tell.

The taxing of capital gains and dividends is substantially lower than the taxing of income earned from work. Maybe you already knew this, maybe you didn't, but this is one huge reason the phrase *the rich just get richer* exists. The tax code is chock full of loopholes that allow for the minimization of taxes paid, and the well-educated or more often the well-educated, advanced-degree professionals such as accountants and attorneys that the wealthy employ understand best how to take advantage of those loopholes. And *loophole* is not a dirty word, my friends. The loopholes are legal. They *are purposeful means of tax avoidance*. Purposeful. So, let's not get all pissy at those who utilize the system to their advantage. If you want to get mad at anything, get mad at the system. Get mad at the buckets.

"Buckets? But I really like buckets."

Do you now?

EARNED. PORTFOLIO. PASSIVE. Those are the three income buckets the IRS is concerned with. Learn them, live them, love them. Okay, you don't really have to love them. Let's take them one at a time.

EARNED INCOME: Money derived from paid work. If you receive a W-2 for work you do, federal and state taxes are taken out automatically from your paycheck. And if you receive a 1099, then it's your responsibility to pay the federal and state taxes. But either way, it's always lots of federal and state taxes. A higher percentage of taxes than the other two buckets, and that's really what we are talking about here. In case you missed it, here's the key line from a few paragraphs ago: *the taxing of capital gains and dividends is substantially lower than the taxing of income earned from work.* Only seven states do not charge income tax: Alaska, Florida, Nevada, South Dakota, Texas, Washington, and Wyoming, and New Hampshire and Tennessee also have versions of no income tax. Those states make up for the lack of income taxes in several other ways, such as toll roads and higher property taxes and sales taxes. The bottom line is that, one way or another, the taxman cometh. Still, he cometh much less for the investors of the world.

PORTFOLIO INCOME: Basically, stocks, bonds, mutual funds, and annuity investments. First you get taxed on your income, then you or your employer parse out a little of what's left to retirement accounts like 401(k)s, the money is given to retirement adviser companies who earn fees for investing it for you, and then they diversify it into stocks, bonds, mutual funds, and annuities. Hopefully, one day those investments have generated enough money so you can retire comfortably on the investment earnings... after paying taxes on those portfolio earnings, of course. Less tax than on your work income but, depending on time frames and types of investments, still plenty in taxes.

[Shaking my head in disgust]

Okay, the specific scenario I painted is not the only way portfolio income is financially flexed, but it is definitely the most prevalent. It is also not how the wealthy get wealthier.

PASSIVE INCOME: This is how the motherfucking wealthy get motherfucking wealthier. What a great word *passive* is. Defined as *accepting or allowing what happens or what others do, without active response or resistance.* Essentially, "Mailbox Money."

"Meaning?"

Meaning, the money just shows up in your mailbox with minimal effort on your part. You go to sleep and wake up and there's some extra money in your account. Or you go out for pizza with your kids, come home, grab the mail, and, *bam*, there's a nice passive income check for you to cash when you're finished racing Formula One cars the following day. Real estate investing and private lending are two great examples of passive income generators. And then there are the loopholes that minimize the taxes you pay on this passive income.

"Okay, great, now how do I personally get rich?"

Good one!

"No, seriously. How do I loophole into some serious retirement wealth?"

Do I look like a wealth manager to you? We're not going to get into the loopholes (it's pretty intense and involves too much further conversation about the tax code, types of retirement accounts, types of ways to file taxes, and the new tax law that passed at the end of 2017, among many other intensities). Not to mention I am not licensed for that kind of advice dispensing. So, instead, we're going to loop back around to the point I'm conveying about all of this in the first place—the money is backward.

I am not only a landlord, but I am also still a renter myself.

"Seriously?"

Well, consider that in 2008 I had debts above my eyeballs as well as deeds and mortgages on some seriously defunct housing in Syracuse and Saint Louis. It took many a year to settle those debts and acquire a personal ledger in the black again. Couple that with building a book of business and paying for an engagement ring, part of a wedding, the honeymoon, new rental properties, having a kid, and simply living in a major metropolitan city without going into debt again, then yes, seriously. Finally, let's not forget about the astounding escalation of real estate prices since 2012. It's only in the last few years that we've been able to even think about purchasing a primary residence, and as my wife has had to listen to me complain about time and again, there is just no way we are doing that now that home prices have skyrocketed again.

Million-dollar properties in okay parts of Los Angeles (referencing school systems here) that will most likely need upgrading or square footage additions to accommodate a growing family are the norm now, and we're not taking on that kind of debt load. Do I sound like a pompous ass kvetching about a problem millions of other Americans could only dream about having? Maybe, but this is my reality, everyone has their own, and we'll touch more on this later, I promise. Plus, whether you are trying to find footing in a city like Los Angeles or figuring out how to put it all together in, say, Raleigh or Dubuque we are all essentially in the same boat when it comes to generating more income and trying to pay less tax on said money.

This does not fall on the One Percent. Our fiscal responsibilities, understanding of tax implications, personal culpability to fend for ourselves and amass our own nest eggs have nothing to do with Frankenstein's Monster.

"But I heard Abigail Johnson is worth over $15 billion now as president and CEO of Fidelity Investments!"

Good for her.

"But, but, Giancarlo Stanton gets over $25 million a year just to be a designated hitter!"

Good for him.

Let it go. Let's look elsewhere for reasons why the middle class is shrinking, not specifically at the people who are rising to the top of the economic food chain. Because in a capitalist civilization, someone (or at least a few people) inevitably rises to the top. That does not make them disgusting leviathans, nor does it mean they are specifically liable for the ever-growing disparity in wealth. Look elsewhere.

We have allowed for the privatization and subsequent profiting off of some of our most fundamental institutions. Backward.

We tax earned income of individuals at a rate that is shockingly higher than the rate applied to corporations, and even more shocking we tax earned income at a higher rate than portfolio and passive income. Double backward.

And we have enabled a supposedly private, but totally government-controlled central banking system to run the entire circus. A circus that boasts some of the most warped acts in economic history, I might add: government-sponsored enterprise (GSE) conservatorships, gargantuan bailouts for institutions deemed too big to fail, excessive amounts of quantitative easing, nearly eight years of a zero-interest rate policy, and, my personal favorite, vampire entitlement programs. Infinitely backward!

"Gross! But what are we going to do about it?"

What do you think we should do about it?

"I don't know. Vote better? Run for office ourselves? Read this chapter fourteen straight times so we sound like educated, but totally arrogant shitheads at small social gatherings?"

We're going to do nothing.

"What the—?"

You do not need to leave your room. Remain sitting at your table and listen. Do not even listen, simply wait, be quiet, still and soli-

tary. The world will freely offer itself to you to be unmasked. It has no choice. It will roll in ecstasy at your feet.

Franz Kafka said that.

"I'm not sure I understand."

Hanged Man superbly illuminates the importance of paradox, and Hanged Man is a magnificent guide on our journey of self-discovery. But above all else, Hanged Man learns to let go by virtue of patience. To hang yourself upside down in order to gain knowledge the likes of Odin's, letting go by being patient will ensure the victory I promised you when we first met.

"Is this a test? This is a test, right? I'm supposed to do something now."

Patience.

"But the Federal Reserve?"

Patience.

"But the cacophony of misinformation loudening by the day?!"

Patience.

"And just when I was starting to like you…"

Shh. Listen.

"I…"

Do not even listen, simply wait, be quiet, still and solitary.

"……………………………………………"

Good.

Remember, certitude is supreme, vulnerability is strength, and the survival of human existence is what matters most. We are now officially in this together.

CHAPTER FOUR

A GENERATION COLLABORATOR

The children now love luxury; they have bad manners, contempt for authority; they show disrespect for elders and love chatter in place of exercise. Children are now tyrants, not the servants of their households. They no longer rise when elders enter the room. They contradict their parents, chatter before company, gobble up dainties at the table, cross their legs, and tyrannize their teachers.

—Unknown

"UNKNOWN SAID THAT?"

Yes, well, the quote is often attributed to Socrates, but its origins cannot be entirely confirmed. Though, assuming Socrates did utter these words at some point between 470 and 399 BCE, we can all agree that a long-ass time has elapsed between then and now. Well over two thousand years, in fact. And what we can surmise, from this quote and from that length of time, is this: for quite a while now, every elder generation has believed that all subsequent generations are disobedient fuckwads. Let it be known that I do not feel this way.

There are seven living generations in the United States.

- The GI Generation, aka the Greatest Generation
- The Mature/Silent Generation
- Baby Boomers
- Generation X
- Millennials
- Centennials
- Generation Alpha

The last of the GI Generation was born in 1925, so the youngest of their ilk is currently ninety-four. That doesn't really leave many ambassadors having a say in our society anymore, though we can certainly pay them their due for the legacy they leave behind. Namely, that so many of them weathered the Great Depression and emerged victorious from World War II. History has produced boundless despots, but few will hold a candle to Adolf Hitler. His reign happened at a time when civilization had already been Westernized, and still, he managed to conquer much of Europe, align himself with an Asian accomplice, and exterminate millions with such precision, such calculated venom, that the reverberations of his actions will be felt for centuries—fucking cock that he was. When the last of the Greatest Generation has perished, even fewer Holocaust survivors will remain. Let's pledge their memory always will.

The oldest of the Mature/Silents also felt the pangs of the Great Depression. The youngest were born just as War World II was ending. And with accolades to Fats Domino and his transcendent "Blueberry Hill," Bill Haley and The Comets' "Rock Around the Clock" (the oft-cited indicator of when rock and roll truly landed) was a chart-topping hit in 1955, so the oldest members of this generation would have been twenty-eight at the time, and the youngest, eleven, when music began changing the world. There was a clear division of races and citizen rights, and everyone in this generation experienced the explosion of television, automobiles, and job growth. Did everyone from this generation experience equal benefits of that growth? Let me save you the suspense—no, they did not.

The Baby Boomers. The Me Generation. If ever there was a generation Socrates would have deplored, it would be this one. Through the decades, they were Greasers and Hippies and Yuppies. The last of the generation was born in 1964, and presently being only fifty-five, that's still plenty young in this current age of technological and medical advancements. They were (are) massive, with nearly seventy-five million members, and those have been retiring in droves for some time now, boosting an explosion in the superannuation living and healthcare economies. They were the pioneers in women's rights and in starting to accept homosexuality, and they were the first to embrace divorce as an acceptable ending to an unhappy marriage. They detonated unto the world with their parents rejoicing that World War II was over, and they've been wreaking havoc ever since. I kid, I kid. Love the Boomers.

Generation X spans the fifteen years between 1965 and 1980. Such an ominous moniker to have bestowed upon your birth. *X*. I am an Xer. From the tail end of the Xers. The term *Generation X* refers to alienated youth, which is fitting since the Me Generation responsible for raising the X Generation was often too busy being the Me Generation so that many Xers felt indelibly alienated. Latch-key kids, as it were. With parents who were either so career driven or just not around anymore (divorce), droves of Xers wore their house key around their neck so they could let themselves in to an empty house after school. Since this generation has been given much grief, it is often broken into two generations: the original Xers followed by the Xennials, born between 1975 and 1985. But we're not going there. It's one generation. A host of other traits associated with Xers make it hard to pin down this sect entirely, which is kind of the point of the name to begin with. We are supposedly cynical and cautious, yet extremely individualistic and entrepreneurial. We're self-absorbed and short on loyalty, but we also love to explore and have a penchant for contribution. *Pffft*. Whatever you say, man.

Generation Y: the Millennials. 1981 to 1995-ish. The coveted demographic of anyone trying to sell anyone anything at any given time now. Cheery, optimistic, focused, respectful, team oriented, schedulers, digitally literate, and, of course…the savior of all humanity—just some of the labels slapped on Millennials. Apparently, Gen X is so venomous that Gen Y is often thought of as a welcomed antidote. Yet it undoubtedly has its pitfalls. Can they really be this cheery? This optimistic? This put together at such a tender age? Or have the pressures placed upon them to usher us all into some new phase of utopia proved too much for them?

We're going to explore Millennials a moment before we move on, because they deserve a little more exploration and because I'm the one doing the writing here. Suffice it to say that they are currently on the tip of the media's tongue at all times, though not necessarily because they are that fascinating, but because it's their turn. Growing up, I vividly recall hearing the never-ending chatter about my own generation, but we all soon enough become old hat when the bright young thing comes clearly into view. And, wow, are Millennials in view at this moment in history.

"You sound kind of jealous of them."

Of course I'm fucking jealous of them! Look how bright and young and thingy they are! But I'm also rooting for them. Big time. Just as I'm rooting for all generations, and all of humanity, for that matter. They only have a few good years left before they are passé like the rest of us, and I really want to give them their due before that happens and the Centennials take over. (No, not in an overlord comic book kind of way—you're thinking of X-Men's Sentinels. Take a step back.) Some demographers want to say this generation started in 1978, but because that would make me a Millennial, I'm kiboshing the notion. I like being a cynical Xer. 1980.

So, let's see, the oldest of them are pushing forty, but the youngest of them will be twenty-three this year. Oh, to be twenty-three again! The Baby Boomers were large in number during their heyday, and it's been estimated that Millennials as a group are equal to if not bigger in size. And, as Generation X was intentionally sliced into two factions, there is a movement to do the same with Millennials: in the original conception, Millennials were born between 1981 and 1995, but in the new categorization Millennials are people born anytime from 1989 to between 1995 and 1997.

Right, this shit all starts to get complicated and confuzzled to the point that it could almost become meaningless. Except, unlike the Generation X split, the Millennial split feels way more understandable. Consider, ARPANET may have been invented in 1983, but the internet went mainstream in 1990 when Tim Berners-Lee gave us the World Wide Web. Which, in terms of historical importance, was basically Johannes Gutenberg in 1439 gifting the world the printing press times, let's say, a hundred billion. Feel me? I say *a hundred billion* is an arbitrarily large enough multiplication factor to boil down how planet-altering the internet has been in comparison to anything else. The bottom line being, Millennials were born before the World Wide Web, and some after. No other living generation can claim such a huge happening to divide their numbers. Computers, satellites, moon landings, two world wars, the Cold War, smartphones, and even 9/11 be damned—the invention of the World Wide Web itself takes all cake. Then eats it too.

"Wonderful imagery and all, but that still doesn't REALLY make them that special."

Maybe not, but this does.

Millennials are the first generation to expand beyond the United States. It's not unheard of to describe people of this certain age in Uruguay or Yemen or Indonesia as Millennials. No way that happens without communicating the major common thread (born right the fuck when they were) that shrinks the world down to the size it is now. Sure, you can find articles on German "Baby Boomers" or "Gen Xers," but those labels were placed as an afterthought once the internet was up and thriving. Prior to the internet, the German Generation Xers were known as the Golf Generation. In Brazil? The Coca-Cola Generation. In Japan? The Lost Generation. Then the internet comes along, and those generations are rebranded as Generation X. Just as postinternet youth are essentially collectively known as Millennials. Even in Timbuktu. That's some powerful shit right there. And it really starts to explain why expectations of Millennials are riding so high—the whole world is not only watching but also participating.

I work with mostly Millennials. Let me amend that. I have my own office cubicle in a WeWork building where the tenants and front desk personnel are all essentially Millennials. They flutter about me like an even merrier, more dramatic version of the Ice Capades is going on outside my glass office window. Okay fine, so plenty of them seem sullen and keep to themselves, but as for most of them, I like their energy, and I feed off their kinetic momentum. I also try to speak to as few of them as possible.

What? I got things to do, people. I can't be sitting around nattering about Netflix binges or why Instagram Stories is way better than Snapchat. I don't kid, I don't kid. Fine, they don't all talk like that, and my wife is an honored Millennial, so let's not get me in too much trouble here. Plus, I'll admit plenty of productive commerce is going on around the building daily as well. And yet, I find myself feeling sympathetic to their plight as redeemers way more than I believe they will bring any more redemption than any other generation. And I don't even need to interact with them to feel this. In such respects I am their coworker, their confederate, their colleague. I am proudly…their collaborator.

For starters, how so many twenty- and thirtysomethings are embracing communal living because they must and then convincing themselves it is super awesome appears to be a bigger problem than we all want to admit. Talk about selling them anything at any given time, this is now happening, and it is a dangerous fallacy. It's one thing to collaborate at a WeWork, but it's quite another to then go home at night to three roommates, as opposed to just one or even zero, while doubling that invasion of personal space by also returning to a home in a communal living community. This isn't the Middle Ages we're living in.

"You kind of have me thinking we'd be better off if it was!"

Patience, young Skywalker.

"Grrrrrrrrrrrrr."

Back to this "cohousing" movement. It is being neatly packaged as a really good alternative to the current housing crisis as opposed to what it really represents: communism.

"Oh crap, here we go again."

Round and round, my friends. Cycles inside of cycles.

"But, come now. A bunch of broke students, graduates, and twenty-somethings just getting started in life who huddle together into living quarters to save a few bucks is communism come home to roost?"

You think being another generation's collaborator also makes me a conspiracy theorist, don't you?

"No comment."

I may be romantic for revolutions, but not the questionable revolutions. Not the Bolshevik Revolution. Not communism. As stated with great aplomb previously, never effing communism. And sadly, faulty propositions like Marxism can all too easily become a way of life when you begin squeezing the national youth into living arrangements like these. Especially when other living arrangements become unaffordable, and especially when it's being spun as the positive these development projects would have you believe. Because as the current housing crisis deepens, as homelessness and its ill effects spiral out of control, and we push our youth toward a new reality of habitation, we risk sowing a seed of revolution that will grow. We are risking *homeownership* becoming a dirty word. We are risking a foundational piece of capitalism going by the wayside. And we are at grave risk of speeding up the process of creating a false Shangri-La way before we are ready to embrace how a real Shangri-La might work.

And yet, housing is not the only threat menacing Millennials, or the rest of us, for that matter. The United States has been moving away from manufacturing for decades and focusing on industries of service instead. Well, guess what? Now over a hundred million Americans work in private service-providing industries, and 70 percent of Americans also don't like their jobs. At least they otherwise could have held government jobs with good pensions when that was still a viable option. Entertainment outlets are either so expensive (live sporting and concert events come to mind) or so diluted (*Star Wars* will be spun-off and remade how many times forever now?) or so curated to the point of exhaustion (Instagram, YouTube, Facebook, whatever) that it's becoming increasingly hard to pretend artistic ingenuity is alive and well. Pics, GIFs, memes, and videos can certainly satiate the ravenously starved for entertainment for generations in perpetuity, but at what cost?

"The cost of a monthly cell phone bill, apparently."

Adorable.

Daily levity is wonderful, but when those same outlets become the primary forms of communication, often taking the place of live physical discussion, or worse, live physical interaction of any sort, where do you think that leaves us?

"I'm guessing not in a great place."

No, not in a terribly a great place.

Dripping water hollows out stone. Not through force, but through persistence. Simple in its truth, elegant in its foreshadowing, this Roman proverb popularized by the poet Ovid is an apt warning about how too much of anything can be dangerous.

"This is where you're going to cheer me up though, right?"

Moi? Here's a way better crew to put a smile on your face:

Dr. Leana Wen, Tarana Burke, Anthony Romero, Christiane Amanpour, Mos Def, Patrick Fitzgerald, Michelle Obama, Susan Jacoby, Marques Brownlee, Janet Mock, Marc Freedman, Malala Yousafzai, Bill Nye, Melissa Harris-Perry, Geena Rocero, Eric Lipton. This is just a short list of people currently worthy of some general admiration and auditory time. They are out there. Dozens, hundreds, thousands more of their ilk. None of them billionaires.

"I thought you also liked the One Percent?"

Liked? What I like is miscellany. Mélange. Salmagundi. Diversity. I like when the media sees past self-aggrandizing politicians and the super-rich white boys' club consisting of Musk, Buffet, Branson, Gates, Bezos, and Zuckerberg as our default statespersons. I like anything that isn't repetitive homogeny meant to dull our senses and wear away our inner stone. I like knowing that Millennials, the supposed saviors of humanity, are truly as individualistic and manifold as they are being told they are. Our future depends on it.

"Perpetuate Tomorrow?"

You are starting to see the light.

"It's less glaring than I thought it would be."

Most things are.

Generation Z. Centennials. Let's pinpoint them as born from 1996 to 2009. Those paying close enough attention will notice a trend of ever-diminishing time spans for these generations. Baby Boomers spanned roughly twenty years, and Centennials span fewer than fifteen years. Perhaps the reduced time spans are necessary to match their attention spans. Levity!

"If you say so."

The first thing anyone seemingly LOVES to talk about regarding Centennials is that each and every one of them was born after the invention of the first smartphone, which arrived between 1992 and 2000, depending on who wins a dull argument between manufacturers. Let's just call it 1995. This is a cool distinction, no doubt, but it is not iGen's (another term for Centennials) main distinction. Diversity is their main distinction. More specifically, less Caucasian, more of everyone else. The tipping point is ever closer, and maybe soon we can rid ourselves of another impeding word that hinders progression far more than most: *minority*. Such a grotesque and wasteful word. Such a pointed reminder aimed at too many people who are constantly and undeservedly retold they don't represent the greater number. Fuck that stupid word. Racial parity is necessary for our survival as a species and Generation Z brings us yet one step closer to this equivalence. I am proudly iGen's collaborator as well.

I questioned the ability of Millennials to exude so much maturity at such a tender age, but so many Centennials seem to care not for my questions. So many of them are collectively proving (at least in this country) to effuse wisdoms unheard of in adolescence. It's one thing to be the annoying, precocious child on a TV show, but how are so many of these youngsters coming off as nonirritating and cogent voices of reason? Rookies and second-year professional athletes (the National Basketball Association especially comes to mind) who are Centennials are carrying themselves like refined veterans. And the Parkland students? Kudos to Parkland students and other like-minded students in every state, taking a stand! They mobilized a massive national protest in just a little over a month, and those protests produced results—advertisers dropping TV personalities and chain stores no longer carrying certain kinds of weaponry. That is an excitingly new kind of power.

Of course, there is a dark side to all this. Like anything, there is a cost, and the devil must be paid, no doubt. Not all of them are mature. Not all of them are adapting to life outside of their avatars well at all. Fair or unfair, Centennials are synonymous with screen time, synonymous with the farthest reaches of social media, and synonymous with security and stability. Yes, that is their pigeonhole as a collective. The need for security and stability.

"Well, those don't sound like such terrible things to be needy about."

True, until you consider why it is they crave such protections.

By the time the Great Recession hit in 2008, a prodigious number of them were already of tender ages between six and twelve. More advanced, more precocious, more developed mentally than previous generations or not, TENDER is the operative word. Far too tender to mentally process the toll the recession had on so many parents and siblings. Just as too many of them are now dealing with an absurd abundance of parents, or siblings, or themselves who are hooked on opioids or prescription drugs or both.

The perceived threat of terrorism is shoved down their collective throats by a twenty-four/seven news cycle, and no parent can reasonably stop that from seeping in. They are bombarded with such a dizzying array of information at all times that a term had to be coined: Infocalypse.

"Aren't we all bombarded by this dizzying array of information now?"

Yes, but not all of us are still mentally developing adolescents, and not all of us were born after the advent of the first smartphone either. Which really means that their youthfulness and understanding of technology give them an edge to probe deeper into cyberspace, deeper into social media outlets, deeper into digital gaming, deeper into virtual reality, and deeper into mainframe landscapes than anyone who came before them. And the syndicated knowledge it takes to stop them from doing this will absolutely be inferior to their knowledge of how to press onward. Now combine their precocity with what they are finding out there, and what will they relentlessly crave most? Assuredly, security and stability.

"Are you sure we can't shield them from all this?!"

Hahahaha! Solid levity yourself. But one thing we can do is finally take a long, hard look at our educational systems. We can abet and ultimately aid the remaining Centennials, and future generations, with a better road map for the journey into adulthood. There are six basic types of schools in the United States.

"Please tell me you're not going to list them all and then do that cheeky breakdown thing of yours for all of them."

No, no, no, no. Definitely not. I'm going to list them all and then do that really important, really self-serving breakdown thing. "Cheeky." How dare you!

Public, private, magnet, charter, online, home.

PUBLIC SCHOOL: Remember when this wasn't a dirty word?

"Two words."

[Unamused blank stare]

"Just saying."

You may think I'm going to shit on public schools, but there will be no shitting upon here. Yes, I am disappointed far too many of them still allow morning prayer...pardon...the Pledge of Allegiance. And, yes, I am dismayed far too many curriculums are still outdated, preparing those learning said curriculums to be overtaken by robots slightly before the rest of us. It's true! I fibbed earlier, the Sentinels are absolutely coming for us all!

"I honestly can't tell if you're kidding or not."

Which is exactly why you're going to keep on reading. Seriously, though, public schools are and will remain our most important means of education for the foreseeable future.

For starters, there is a downward trend in private school attendees, which inversely means that the public school population is growing, and it was already pretty freaking big to begin with. Like 75 percent of total schools and 90 percent of all school attendees big.

"And the money?"

Oh, what a question at just the right time! You are starting to get me, good people. The cartouche, the graticule, the rectification of it all. What about the money, indeed. Thirty-six percent of most state budgets and 8.5 percent of the federal budget pay for public schooling K–12. And because public schooling is the kind of constitutionally protected entitlement I clearly advocate, wouldn't it be nice to see those billions of dollars put to their highest and best use? As in, immediately recognizing the gargantuan shift in the overall racial population and massive technological disruption around the bend—assimilating the pedagogy accordingly? Posthaste!

Start with the technology. More technology. Everywhere. All the time. As much as the budgets will allow. And then some. Fund-raise for this nonstop. In every school district. Teachers and parents will have to do their best to monitor (plenty already are), but the more hardware and software integrated into curriculums, the better. There are the obvious reasons for this, such as the innumerable doors that only exposure to technology can open, but it's more than that now. It's also preparation for what's coming down the pike in the coming decades, and it's something we're also going to touch on further a little later. But for the time being? Double, no, octuple the school budgets. Hell, cut the national military spending in half. Cut the seventeen national security institutions down to six. Immediately raise Social Security benefits to seventy-five years old, and redirect every dollar saved to education. More specifically, redirect most of those dollars to education equality over racial and social divides. You heard me correctly, give most of the money to nonwhite school districts and any rural or urban neighborhoods below the poverty line. No, I'm not condescendingly promoting some sort of pity charity; I'm supporting a tipping of the scales until they can tip themselves back to impartiality. You want condescension?

"Not particularly."

A little bit coming anyway…

If you are teaching "Intelligent Design," stop. If your lunch lines serve more processed crap than fresh fruits and vegetables, stop. If you are reluctant to share your school's or school district's instructive data for fear it will reflect poorly on you or your communities, stop. If you are employing anyone other than a competent comptroller (even if it means outsourcing) to endlessly make tough decisions and reduce fixed costs, stop. If it's obvious that you reside in a district where the benefits of year-round school vastly outweigh summer break disadvantages, but you are still encouraging the break, stop. If you are not tirelessly tinkering with energy, consumption, and transportation conservation methods for your school and still want to call yourself educators, do so. Tomorrow.

There are so many great teachers, administrators, and parents in the public school realm who understand that education is not everything, it's the only thing. They are underpaid, overworked (millions have heroically taken on second jobs just to make ends meet on an educator's salary), and drowned out by the "let me justify my position" bureaucrats of the world, and it hurts so badly that I legitimately feel it in my testes.

"Did we really need that image?"

I'm not even going to do that denigrating world ranking thing and tell you that the United States sits somewhere between tenth and twenty-fifth on every list. Or did I just do that? We especially reek at math. Deplorable!

"Okay, okay. But are you going to disappoint us now and admit you're a private school kid, or are you even a public school product yourself?"

You bet your ass I'm a public school product. Loud and proud. And that includes a public university for college, don't forget.

PRIVATE SCHOOL: I have plenty of love for private schools too. They are both vast in method and vast in form. Some are boarding, some are parochial, some are language immersion. Some utilize Montessori methods, others like Reggio Emilia, and still others prefer, well, any number of additional methods. And why not? For your money you should get what you pay for. Private schools don't get tax dollars, they get hardworking parent dollars, which is what needs to be left over to be able pay for these expensive schools after taxes are paid. There's not much that needs to be said about private schooling other than that. If you have the means and you want your child to attend a military academy that focuses on teaching geopolitics, I'm not going to pretend I agree with that line of thinking, but still, bully for you.

"Do you think private schools are really better than public schools?"

Absolutely not, but plenty of them are, and much of that "better" depends a great deal on the aforesaid issues with public schools compared to private school offerings.

HOME SCHOOL:

"I think you skipped over a few."

I think you're right, but we're going to come back to them in a minute. I'm putting homeschooling here because it coincides nicely with private schooling. Mostly because it's hard to argue with its merits.

"I beg to differ."

As would a lot of people, but they'd be missing the point. Homeschooling is a line-in-the-sand choice.

"Not necessarily the kid's choice."

No, but they don't get a choice.

"*Gasp.*"

Gasp all you want, but let's stop pretending that outside of them having some say in their own curriculums, that kids do or even should get a choice. Parents make the choices until the kid is old enough and educated enough to make decisions on their own that will ultimately affect society. As it is now, there exists a type of schooling known as homeschooling, and if the rules for said schooling are followed, there will exist a recognition of a completed degree by the homeschooled. And much like public or private or any other type of schooling, some parents and communities are going to do a hell of a job homeschooling their kids, and others aren't. And some homeschooled kids are going to be just fine integrating socially, and others aren't. Regardless, those degrees are going to be recognized, so we should welcome any who have one, just like degrees from any other type of schooling.

MAGNET SCHOOL: I could have lumped these next to public schools because they are, in fact, public. But in contrast to standard public schools, they offer specialized courses that often attract students from other schools' zones, hence the term *magnet.* They became popular in the 1970s as a way to fight racial segregation in public schools. Really, in that decade several avenues, known as the Open Schools approach, fought racial segregation, but magnet schools have been the most successful of those initiatives and remain a viable option today. Their success results largely from the thoughtful blending of students' cultural backgrounds and socioeconomic statuses and the schools marketing themselves as providing a higher standard of education through competition. Imagine that, entrance exams, interviews, auditions (and lotteries) for admission into a system that pares down its focus to a few disciplines. Why, that sounds a bit like life after high school in a capitalist society. I can't fathom why these magnet schools are thriving. Can't fathom at all.

"Well, there has to be some downside to these schools, right?"

No, they are perfect in every respect. Absolute perfection. *Whistling...whistling...*you're not buying that, are you? Fine. For one, they often pull the top percentage of students away from their own neighborhood schools, which inevitably leaves a void in that neighborhood school, where the bar is lowered, and the more average students suddenly become the top percentage, and that's not who they really are. So now those students are feeling unwarranted pressure to achieve, and the other students in the lower percentage have also lost an entire segment of peers to look up to. And those lost peers, who could otherwise have helped pull those students up given enough time (say, a decade in an appropriately funded school system, with appropriately paid, highly motivated teachers), are now gone. *Poof*—enrolled in a magnet school.

But is that really on the magnet school? Or is that on our own deficiencies as a country not homed in nearly enough on education? I have no problem being a broken record…not nearly enough state and federal money, not nearly enough compensation to educators, not nearly enough distribution of wealth to economically depressed neighborhoods, not nearly enough tools/resources/time/care given to neighborhood public schools. Octuple the efforts.

CHARTER SCHOOL: Oh, shit. It was only one chapter ago you heard me railing against the privatization of what should otherwise be public institutions. Here we go again. Technically, charter schools are public schools, because they receive government funding AND are open to all students AND do not charge tuition. Then again, technically, the New York Jets are considered a professional franchise because they are members of the National Football League. Do you at least like that wraparound humor?

"Not really."

Tough crowd today!

Intrinsically, I do not want to have an issue with charter schools. They are, after all, schools. And there are plenty of wonderful teachers, administrators, students, and parents affiliated with charter schools around the country at this very moment. An ample number of them offer fine curriculums, and really, any establishment designated for the purposes of education is an establishment I always want to root for.

"But you're not rooting for them?"

Oh, I'm rooting for them, all right. But like my beloved New York Jets, I'm rooting for them cautiously.

Three concepts have carried them from their inception in the 1970s well into the 2000s (opportunity, choice, results responsibility) and seemingly played a big role in why Bill Clinton, George W. Bush, and Barack Obama called for their expansion. You may have noticed them popping up in almost every major city today? Also, as usual, there's the money.

Now, with no apologies to cotton, we know money is the real fabric of our lives, and those who profit from charter schools can too easily convolute the money. Businesses can start charter schools. That's right. Not just parents, community leaders, teachers, or school districts. Businesses, too. This is where we are right now. Corporations can be construed as individuals thanks to the *Citizens United* Supreme Court ruling in 2010, and businesses can lobby to charter a school. See any conflict of interest there? No? Then you must run a fucking super-PAC.

Public K through 12 schooling cannot, shall not, must not be about profit.

"Hold it. Back it up. Stop spouting. Time the eff out again!"

By all means, I love a good interruption.

"I'm paying very close attention like you asked me to, and now I'm struggling, Pfeffer. I'm struggling with your calls for outsourced comptrollers to run public school budgets while at the same time voicing disdain for privatization. I'm struggling with your fascination with capitalism while you speak out of both sides of your mouth about money. And I'm really struggling to understand how you are a landlord yourself yet deplore the idea that a private individual could be the landlord for a state-funded school."

Wow, I hadn't even gotten to that point about charter schools yet, but great inference by you.

So, TRADE and INDUSTRY are the basic institutions of capitalism from which private operators can profit, agreed? Government should be there to encourage the never-ending expansion of these institutions, but mostly, our government should be concerned with the other institutions that protect unalienable rights to life, liberty, and a pursuit of happiness. Those institutions are EDUCATION, HEALTH CARE, INFRASTRUCTURE, NATIONAL SECURITY, and DEMOCRACY. All seven institutions obviously need money to function. The first two should circulate the money privately and ultimately keep the money private. The last five institutions should get the money from taxing the profits that the private money created.

But we know better. We know that is not what has transpired over the course of our nearly two hundred fifty years of existence as a country. We have meddled, we have muddled, we have corrupted, and we have bowed at the feet of false idols. We have painted ourselves into a corner, and now we make it worse by constructing mousetraps to get ourselves out instead of simply letting the paint dry first.

"And this is why we've had to concoct yet another mousetrap like, say, charter schools? To try to get out of the corner we painted ourselves into by woefully screwing up our standard public education system?"

Truth is at once exquisite and painful, no?

Shiiiiiiiit.

ONLINE SCHOOLS: We are there.

"Where?"

The same place Robert Johnson sold his soul to the devil to play the guitar the way he could, of course. At the crossroads!

1994: CALCampus. 1997: California Virtual University. 1999: Jones International University accreditation. 2002: MIT OpenCourseWare Project. Clearly, online education has been around for some time, except…

"Except what?"

Except those were college-based initiatives. In fact, tell me when you read the words *online school* you didn't immediately think of a higher learning?

"I really did."

Online technical schools. Online trade accreditations. Online college degrees. Not anymore. The last decade has seen the emergence of cyberschools K–12. And much like cyberspace itself, a deep dive into cyberschooling for all could send us spinning off in a million directions. Well, we're only interested in one direction. Forward.

"Usually, when you say something like that you're about to take me backward."

It's nice getting to know each other so intimately, I have to say.

Earlier in the public school paragraph I promised we'd revisit technology. Well, that time is nigh.

"Seriously, who talks like that?"

Lofted assholes, that's who.

"Seriously lofted."

Half of all current human jobs are going to become obsolete in the coming decades.

"Holy crap, man, maybe a little warning before dropping a bomb like that?!"

Best to just rip off the Band-Aid while you were distracted.

"Freaking Sentinels, man. They really are coming for us. But half?"

Pretty damn close to half. Maybe more. Which means ALL of the current educational curriculums and technologies being taught in every type of school need some serious updating, pronto. Like, remember the founding principles of charter schools? Opportunity, Choice, Results Responsibility. Yeah, well when the machines come for 50 percent of the world's workforce over the next twenty-five years, those principles will roughly translate to *Blah, Blech*, and *Barf.*

"Please tell me you've got some better principles to share!"

Critical Thinking, Community, Collaboration, Creativity. Also known as the Four Cs of Twenty-First-Century Learning, they are the product of a range of entities (nonprofits, governmental agencies, academic associations, etc.) that recognized the need for a better way forward in the age of burgeoning artificial intelligence. So, yes, a movement is already under way, and, yes, plenty of schools, charter schools included (lest anyone admonish me for making it seem like they are out of touch), are already adopting these principles.

"Although, am I crazy, or does it seem like grade schools get a new acronym with each incoming White House administration that aims to fix the problem?"

I wouldn't call you crazy, no. It does seem like that. And there have already been calls by some to add a fifth *C*. And not just one specific *C*, mind you. Cultural Competence, Connections, Career Readiness, and, my personal favorite, Climate have all been floated. Still, consider that all previous attempts at skill set adjustments operated under the belief that though the world was ever changing, half of everyone on the planet who worked could still, you know, expect to keep their job and not be totally displaced by the momentous global rift that is climate change. Welcome to the twenty-first century, good people.

"You're still not funny. Also, the last of the Millennials are already eighteen and out of grade school, and the last of the Centennials will probably be aged out before the widespread adoption of these principles, so most of our supposed saviors might have missed the boat on this one."

Enter the next supposed saviors...

Generation Alpha. They are so fresh, so new to the world that Wikipedia does not yet have a page about them. The first of them were born in 2010, and who knows when the last will be born? But, assuming a recent trend of fifteen-year generations, that would put the last of them coming to a planet near you in 2025. That's six years from now. A lot can happen in six years, and it will be another ten years after that before the last of them emerge as young adults.

My son is an Alpha. Okay, you got me, I absolutely love the sound of that! Two and a half million of them are being born around the world every week. Do you like simple equations? Me too. Two and a half million times fifty-two weeks is 130 million. Times another seven years is nearly 1 billion people. And let's not forget about the nearly 1 billion of them that have already been born in the last nine years. That's over a quarter of Earth's current population being added to the mix over a fifteen-year period. No biggie. It only took tens of thousands of years to get to 7.5 billion people...shouldn't be a problem to add nearly 30 percent on top of that number over a fifteen-year period, right?

"Well, what about all the people who are going to die over that fifteen-year span as well?"

Just seeing if you were still paying attention. So, it only ends up being half a billion people added. A mere 6.5 percent increase. I think I read somewhere that we totally have the resources and greenhouse capacity to accommodate that kind of bump.

"Up yours and your eye roll."

Indeed.

India will soon overtake China as the most populous country on Earth with the help of this generation. The world's Muslim population will grow twice as fast as the number of non-Muslims over the life span of Alphas. And in the United States, total Caucasian representation will slip below 60 percent for the first time ever after Alphas are done being born. These are scary figures for some, quite exhilarating for others, but they are merely statistics that distract us all from the real test that demands our focus.

Understanding and ultimately digesting the advancements is the real test. The Baby Boomers had the space race. The Xers had computers. The Millennials had the internet. The Centennials had smartphones. Three generations before Baby Boomers were the Hard Timers, born between 1890 and 1908. Plenty of them lived long enough to see the race to space, which must have seemed downright fucking incredible compared to the biggest advancements of the nineteenth century: steam engines, locomotives, the telephone, combustible engines, electricity. Just as the remaining major advancements in the twentieth century must have: airplanes, automobiles, television, computers, rocketry, nuclear power, antibiotics, the internet. And here we are in just the beginning part of the twenty-first century and half the world's population now has a miniaturized computer in their pocket, with countless applications at their fingertips. This is indisputably something most Baby Boomers would have been baffled by if you showed them a smartphone anytime in the 1960s.

"Will Millennials and Centennials be just as baffled when the miniaturized computers in their pocket advance rapidly enough to take over their careers soon?"

That's going to depend on them.

Consider, the crux of the scientific revolution can be pinpointed to 1543, when Nicolaus Copernicus published his largest work, *De revolutionibus orbium coelestium*, the volume that enlightened the world about the earth revolving around the sun, and not the other way around. Prior to the start of this revolution (one of the good revolutions, I may add), tens of thousands of years of human advancement might best have been described as… lumbering? We'll go with that. And after 1543, just less than five hundred years of human advancement brings about mind-boggling progress by the decade now. So, in some respects, we've recently all been preparing ourselves for the coming rapidity of computer intelligence. Our youth especially.

"That's a whole lot of homogeneity you're accounting for. You, uh, kind of railed against homogeny earlier and touted individualism pretty hard."

Well, now, I can't accuse you of not paying attention, can I?

To your point, definitely peril is implicit in lumping millions, nay, billions of people into tidy bubbles as we have in this chapter. After all, we're all precious snowflakes, aren't we? (Yeah, I just vomited a little in my own mouth too.) But that lumping is the reality of trying to best understand each other. Not every stereotype is evil. Not every overly condensed memorandum need be taken with offense. Like it or not, if you were born in a certain year, you belong to a certain generation. And whether Socrates likes it or not, all subsequent generations will be ever more intertwined around the world, not to mention ever more advanced than the sum of dozens of generations before them.

And here we stand in the throes of advancements of another generation, where in the nine years alone since Alphas started spawning, the Higgs boson particle has been confirmed, 3D printing is a reality, personal drones soar the skies, self-driving cars are officially on the road, and plans to send human ambassadors to Mars are well underway.

It seems reasonable to think virtual reality, bionics, gene splicing, and especially artificial intelligence will be ubiquitous when Alphas become the bright shiny young thing everyone is trying to market to. And though I may be three generations removed, I hope never to get so cranky that they all suddenly appear disobediently fuckwaddish to me. Because when I look at these endearing little growth-spurters now (including my son), I don't see future spoiled brats with impending complexes. Hell, I don't even see the tykes they are just trying to utilize mind-blowing technology like forks and iPads correctly. I see conquerors attempting to master the tools afforded to them. I see victory in self-discoverers who will be making important world decisions for the rest of us soon enough. I see inquisitiveness. I see thriving. I see certitude. I see the best of Hanged Man.

With great pride, I am forever their confidante. I am forever their coworker, their confederate, their colleague. I remain, faithfully, forever their collaborator.

Every last little fuckwad.

CHAPTER FIVE
A SOCIABLE INTROVERT

An introvert was not something you wanted to be during my time of adolescence. The word was co-opted by authority in an effort to shame you into being more jubilant in communal settings. More vibrant at parties. More vocal in school. More proactive on the dating scene. To be livelier at, shucks, everything. Almost as if the main ingredient for quality of life was assimilation with the crowd who was the most boisterous. Sheep assimilate pretty well with their crowd. Eh, maybe not that one black sheep.

Introvert. One definition: *A shy, reticent person.*

"Reticent?"

Not revealing one's thoughts or feelings readily.

Introvert again: *One who prefers to spend time alone in order to recharge their inner being.*

Hmm, I like that second introversion definition the best. I especially like it because, if you couldn't tell, I give zero fucks about sharing my thoughts or feelings readily, though as one who absolutely prefers spending time alone to recharge my inner being, I am most definitely an introvert. A seriously sociable introvert, at that.

Those authority figures throwing around all that shame seem to have calmed the rhetoric quite a bit these days. Let's not be too hard on them, as plenty of authority figures have been wrong before: a consensus of doctors encouraging recreational smoking up until the 1960s, the USDA's first few stabs at the Food Pyramid, the widely held belief that HIV originated from humans fucking monkeys…the list goes on and on. The important thing here is that introverts are finally getting their due because it is accepted now that an introvert's brain simply responds a certain way to dopamine and that their psychological makeup allows them to feel most comfortable in the throes of introspection. Oh, fuck yes, science wins again!

If you ask me (if you're still reading this far, you basically are), the world could use as much introspection and inner-being recharging as we can muster. Everything moves so damn fast now. 4G wireless connections, with 5G coming soon. Twitter Bots and their infectious gossip. Faster delivery services, faster-working drugs, faster transportation, faster ways to hook up. Yes, I am fucking aware I sound old as dirt. I'm also guessing you already know I am bringing this up for a reason, especially after my open love affair with technological advancement last chapter.

"Yeah, you're kind of an open book at this point."

Levity at its best!

As I was saying, the world moves lighting fast, and maybe those who enjoy decompressing with said open book and a glass of something strong on a living room couch by themselves somewhere are on to something. Maybe a little contemplation in a world gone mad is just what the doctor ordered. But maybe not from those thumbs-up-for-smoking doctors.

"Master of the obvious over here. 'Prosper Today'?"

"Did you really just smiley face at me?"

"Seriously, stop that."

My very astute wife likes to poke fun at me for what she calls my affinity for "Lonely Man Art." I consider myself an acutely self-aware person, but this is not a predilection I knew about until she correctly pointed it out. I really do gravitate toward works that romanticize the joys of solitude. I'll walk over hot coals to catch any documentary about a loner and their quest. My musical tastes can best be broken down into three categories: sentimental band, sentimental singer/songwriter, sentimental vocalist in an outdoor marketplace desperately trying to hawk their talents. Any painting depicting a moribund solitary figure? Bring it. *The Old Man and the Sea*? Only the greatest book ever. Even some of my fantasies evoke visions of isolation. I shit you not, I have thought more than once that in a different life it might have been fun to be a Siberian oil guard who spent most of his days playing cards and trying to keep warm via small sips of vodka. I shared this great vision once with my best friend and he looked at me like I imagine you are looking at this book right now. Some fucking best friends you all are!

And yet, I welcome a good social outing too. My days of clubbing into the early morning are over, but you can pretty much bring me anywhere else and I'd be content. Dinners, parties, dinner parties, Universal Studios, Tennessee. I don't know…just spit-balling here. But I'm good with going places, and I like to think I'm good at being brought to said places as well. Maybe it's because of a lifetime of having to accrue confidence (after being born with none), or maybe my days as a bartender helped hone a sorely needed craft, but I don't lack for friends, and my wife has yet to utter the phrase "we never go anywhere anymore." And we have a small child to take care of, so that's a relatively good sign.

It's a balance. As is having a fair number of friends like we do, which in and of itself is a garden that gets tougher to maintain with each passing year. Social media was supposed to be this great boulevard for quickly catching up with acquaintances, but what happens when you don't really partake in social media?

"Surely you jest."

I do not jest, and I'll tell you what happens—you make an effort to call friends on the phone and have close, personal conversations.

"You're right, you are old as dirt."

This is important to me, and anyone who knows me will answer when I call instead of texting me back or Snapchatting me a "sorry, in a meeting right now." I have nothing against social media—

"Yes, you do."

Okay, yes, I do, but my main issue is probably not what you think.

Aside from our recent exposures to the dark side of social media: fake news, public shaming, "Outrage Culture," the deceitful gathering of personal information, et al., the light side of social media is still currently winning out, though it is getting quite close for comfort. We're going to get into much more of this a little later, but it's important to note here that the sharing and caring it was meant for still beats strong, and social media has my vote in abstention for those who enjoy partaking. As for me? I have two personal reasons to stay away.

The first is foot-in-mouth syndrome.

"Is that anything like hoof-and-mouth disease?"

It is not.

"Did you just make up a phony syndrome?"

I can't take credit for making it up, no, but it certainly feels like a real syndrome. Still, it speaks for itself, and five chapters deep like you are now, you can imagine how I might occasionally say something that would rub someone the wrong way. [Cough, cough]

"So? Lots of people take to social media to proverbially rub people the wrong way."

Yes, but they do it purposefully to fill a life void by screaming into an echo chamber. That ain't me. And my days shan't be filled igniting cyber fires just because I enjoy fanning flames.

"And the second?"

The second is my propensity to be swayed by pop culture.

"Oh, this should be interesting."

It is. And so is the irony that those who sell for a living are often the most likely to be sold on something. That's me—a salesperson by trade who is too easily swayed when off duty.

"Like, you have a closet full of two hundred pairs of expensive sneakers or something?"

Not quite. This isn't a consumerism thing. This is a susceptible-to-being-influenced-by-intangible-bright-shiny-objects thing, and social media offers up the brightest and shiniest.

I mentioned earlier that I am acutely self-aware, and this is one facet of my personality that I am well aware of. Another way of looking at it is that I have a Pythagorean theorem problem. Pop Culture (a^2) + Social Media (b^2) = Rabbit Hole (c^2). Breaking this down further, I fucking love pop culture. Too much. Way too much. So much that I have a frightening inclination to be influenced by its cultural dominance, which means it's best for me to avoid its endless tentacles. I'm self-prescribing fresh air for myself here, people.

It used to be a couch potato thing growing up, which was bad enough. But at least television was the only main abusive outlet for junkies such as me to get their pop culture smack. Take me away from the TV and of course my productivity increased dramatically, whereas my daydreaming decreased accordingly.

"Well, daydreaming isn't bad. Studies have shown..."

Yes, yes, I'm aware of the studies, thank you. Just as I am aware daydreaming can be a distinguishing mark of an industrious introvert. Except we're talking about obsessive daydreaming here. I mentioned in the introduction that I am obsessive about the truth, but obsessiveness is not a personality trait you turn on for one thing and turn off for another. If I'm obsessive about the truth, it means I'm obsessive about everything, including pop culture and absolutely including the outlets pop culture gets delivered through. We're not in rural Kansas anymore, Toto, with only one bunny ears television to be found in the living room. We're officially in the future, where the computer and its technological friends are essentially unavoidable. It's my prerogative, nay, my responsibility, nay, my SWORN DUTY to myself and my family to limit the pop culture and its influences over me. Therefore, I voraciously limit the social media by which it is distributed. Bye, Instagram.

I was not just a fantasist growing up, I was a liar too. Oh, you weren't ready to get this deep? That's a shame, we're getting deep. I was a total bullshitter. I bullshitted my parents, my brother, friends, teachers—which inescapably means I constantly bullshitted myself. I was convinced I could bullshit my way through anything, so I did. Sometimes it worked, and most of the time it was amusing (to me at least), but it stunted my maturity by a good decade. Maybe more.

Worse, lying made me crude to other people because I was innately ashamed of the bullshitting I was doing. And that kind of consequent lack of respect for yourself can unfairly get projected onto others. I was not particularly kind to any member of the opposite sex who showed any interest in me, probably because deep down I couldn't understand why they would. I treated service industry personnel poorly, often berating customer service operators, and acted like waitstaff were beneath me. I belonged to a youth group during high school and took positions of power in our chapter to wield that power over other members. How? I hazed younger members to the point of embarrassment. Then in college I did the same thing all over again when I joined a fraternity. Also, while in college, I wasted one semester partying so hard that I got put on academic probation for failing to keep at least a 2.0 GPA, and then I doctored that semester's transcript so the one my parents ended up seeing was a complete fabrication. Their hard-earned tuition dollars put to good use, huh?

And you already know about my early twenties living in Los Angeles…bullshitting my way through Hollywood jobs and writing endeavors and ultimately bleeding cash into real estate investments with no clue what I was doing. Or maybe worse. Maybe deep down I was making those callow real estate choices to unwittingly reprimand myself, ultimately digging myself into the hole I subconsciously thought I belonged in. Maybe there was no maybe about that.

Yep, I was a bullshitter. Not a totally terrible human being, but not a complete one either. Certainly not a mature one. Not until I started working as a bartender that second time.

When I wasn't working at the Marquis, or homing in on real estate opportunities, I was reading. Reading everything I could. Followed by writing again. Free writing. Free thought. Contemplating who I was and my place in this town, this world, this life. I was finally ripening. I even recognized this maturing, because I noticed my fantasies were maturing too. Before the Marquis days,

I would ponder like a pubescent teen might…fetishized sexual encounters or scoring the winning touchdown, sinking the winning basket, making the winning play.

"And the fantasies during your days at the Marquis?"

They evolved. Instead of the winning play and how laid it would get me, I dreamed about what it would be like to be the fourth-rotation pitcher on a marginal team like the Tampa Bay Rays, what I would do with the $8 million a year I'd make to play only twice a week, and how I would juggle the road mistresses waiting for me in Baltimore and Houston.

"Wow, total maturity!"

I said I was matur-ING, not completely mature. Now that I'm officially "old as dirt" and married, I basically just fantasize about moves I'd make if someone were to promote me to general manager of the New York Jets.

"Do the sports world a favor and fold up the franchise and sell the buildings and other departments for scraps?"

That's not funny.

"Yes, it is."

Okay, it's a little bit funny.

Speaking of sports and maturing, I've whittled down my play to three leisure activities: skiing, golf, and tennis.

"No cricket?"

I'm the one doing the comedy here, not you!

"Bah!"

As I was saying, three leisure activities.

"Why?"

For fear of getting hurt, of course. Do you know what the most likely outcome of playing blacktop basketball against other foul-happy forty-year-olds is? Eight weeks of me on crutches trying to keep up with my kid. Pass.

"Skiing can be dangerous."

Sure, when I was twenty and jumping off rocks in the trees. Now it's pretty much *shush*-ing down the middle of intermediate trails wearing a helmet.

"Tennis can be fierce."

Especially the way I play tennis it can be!

"Wait, so you're admitting you're not a complete wimp and still have some fight left in you?"

Not only am I admitting it, but my behavior toward tennis further explains my id, ego, and superego all in one big swing of the bat.

"And now we're mixing sports metaphors for some reason?"

There is great truth to be found in our contradictions.

"Solid one there, Yoda."

☺

"Son of a…!"

I'm a good tennis player. Good, not great. Not playing in weekend tournaments for money great. Not I played in college or could ever have dreamed of sniffing pro or even semi-pro level great. I'm USTA certified 4.0 level (for anyone who knows what that means), and I'm in a recreational doubles league with other like-minded fanatics. But if you were inside my head as I gear up before playing anyone, you might see the neurons in my brain firing at the same level as Rafael Nadal's circa 2008, when he was essentially bionic. I like to think I'm bionic out on the court.

Scratch that. It's worse than that. I like to pretend I'm Frank Castle.

"Who?"

You know, Frank Castle!

"Except I don't know."

The Punisher.

"Um, what the hell are you talking about?"

I'm trying to share with you the image with which I manifest my psychopathic tendencies.

"Ahhhhh. Wait, what?"

Tennis is so much more than a leisure activity for me, my friends. So much more. It is an outlet for the part(s) of this lover of Buddhism that wants to destroy my fellow man violently. And though I am but a mediocre player at best, I treat my opponents like they wiped out my entire family and I have nothing left to live for but exacting the appropriate damage that wiping out my entire family might inspire me to inflict. Or as *The Punisher* comic book slogan states so eloquently: *It's not revenge. It's punishment.*

How dare you make me get out of bed this early and run me around this court wearing such a strange, ostentatious outfit? Punishment. How dare you tear me away from time with my wife and kid and make me sweat this much for two hours? Punishment. How dare you call that serve out when it was clearly fucking in by a fucking mile?! Punishment! On and on it goes. Sometimes I win, sometimes I lose, but always with the punishment.

"You are…not a well individual."

Maybe not, but I'm now honest with myself about said unwellness and why I need tennis as an outlet so badly. That's a big step for me. Just as big a step as recognizing my pop culture addiction, understanding my attraction to unsociable artworks, and ultimately accepting my role as a sociable introvert so that I may use it as necessary to thrive in my daily environment. Thrive we aspire to. Thrive we must. And I am confident the strength derived from exploring my vulnerabilities is a modus operandi I can get behind.

"Huh, maybe you are a well individual."

Maybe each Hanged Man Prospers Today because they are a little of both.

“😊”

There is a devastatingly poetic piece of writing that David Mamet shared in his play *Glengarry Glen Ross*. Okay, so the whole play is poetry, but in the movie version, one scene early on between Al Pacino as the slick Ricky Roma and Jonathan Pryce as the impressionable James Lingk blows me away every time. The psychology of “human capital” is on full display as one man yearns to hold onto his soul while another man seeks to possess it. Lingk is at a Chinese restaurant after work trying to enjoy a quiet drink by himself, but the salesman Roma is imposing his worldview upon him to make a sale. In Mamet’s words:

RICKY ROMA: *All train compartments smell vaguely of shit. It gets so you don’t mind it. That’s the worst thing that I can confess. You know how long it took me to get there? A long time. When you die you’re going to regret the things you don’t do. You think you’re queer? I’m going to tell you something... we’re all queer. You think you’re a thief? So what? You get befuddled by a middle-class morality? Get shut of it. Shut it out. You cheat on your wife? You did it, live with it. You fuck little girls, so be it. There’s an absolute morality? Maybe. And then what? If you think there is, go ahead, be that thing. Bad people go to hell? I don’t think so. If you think that, act that way. A hell exists on earth? Yes. I won’t live in it. That’s me. [Long Pause]. You ever take a dump made you feel like you’d just slept for twelve hours?*

“Well, that was vivid and vulgar.”

I know, but I like to save my apologies for when I really do something wrong, so sorry, not sorry. Renton’s *Trainspotting* diatribe was a savage takedown of how mundane life can be as a member of the middle class, but Roma’s diatribe illuminates something far more relevant to our future, a middle-class morality. An apt microcosm of culture when it was penned in 1984, Mamet’s script is quite possibly even more apt thirty-five years later. As in, there was undoubtedly a middle class in 1984, just as there was the morality that came along with it. Can we say the same about 2019? Will we even know what those words meant in 2050?

Homes, appliances, automobiles. This is a major U.S. mark on the world after nearly two hundred and fifty years. "Conspicuous consumption." *Buying expensive items to display wealth and income rather than to cover the real needs of the consumer.* Herbert Hoover was president for one term during the dog days of the Great Depression in the early 1930s and is most often associated with the term "rugged individualism." *The practice or advocacy of individualism in social and economic relations emphasizing personal liberty and independence, self-reliance, resourcefulness, self-direction of the individual, and free competition in enterprise.* It may have taken fifty years to catch on, but, wow, did Ronald Reagan leverage this notion into a raison d'être for conspicuous consumption during the economic boom of the 1980s.

"And now?"

Now we're still blinging out even though few of us can afford the bill! The United States takes distinct pleasure in showcasing just how large our homes can get, how many appliances we can own, and how many automobiles can fit in our garages. This is what we can boast as the most spotlighted country on earth subscribing to capitalism. Bigger homes, shinier coffee makers, and ALL the Ford F-150s. Lovely. The tenets of the supreme economic and political system have been throttled within our borders, and our leaders are still trying to convince the rest of the world that the dollar should remain the peg as the global exchange rate? Somebody dig up Calvin Coolidge so he can have a good cry already.

Cycling back to the morality part, a "middle-class morality" is hard to formally define, but it's essentially how a middle-class member is expected to behave. Apparently, that behavior should include an insatiable appetite for stuff. For consumption. Here's a stock dividend for you, middle-class investor, now go consume as much plastic as possible so we can not only finally use up fossil fuels but also further contribute to the enormous waste issue that has created climate change. Here's a piddling tax rebate for you, middle-class citizen, now go consume as much cheap processed foodstuffs as possible so you can gain weight and keep our agricultural, pharmaceutical, and health insurance industries humming along. Here's an insufficient biweekly paycheck for you, middle-class worker, now go consume whatever you can on homes, appliances, and cars after spending OVER HALF of that paycheck on basic necessities first. Over half! This is now the scariest threat to the middle class, the cost of basic necessities.

"Are you sure it's not terrorism?"

Now it is you who jests.

"But the Brookings Institute just recently came out with news that half the world's population is now middle class or wealthier. This has to be a good thing!"

Why does it have to be?

"Because that's what we're all striving for, isn't it? A more robust middle class. Well, now we have it, and we have it globally. How does this not excite you?"

Clearly, in all the excitement over the Brookings news you missed what I just said, so we'll try this again. Becoming middle class comes with an anvil of morality. A middle-class morality. A morality that started taking a beating in our own great nation in the 1970s when wage stagnation emerged. How do you think it's going to fare around the rest of the world?

"Wet blanket much, do you?"

Care to answer my question?

"Blah!"

The 1980s may have been fun, but they were a three-ring circus if there ever was one. The first two rings: conspicuous consumption intertwined with rugged individualism. Bad enough, but that third ring of middle-class morality urging everyone to keep up with all that fun was ultimately too much for the stagnated wages to handle. And maybe if the party had stopped there, we could have course-corrected, but the 1990s and 2000s were big economic parties themselves.

"Partying usually comes with a hell of a hangover."

I don't know about you, but I chugged a lot of aspirin right around 2008.

And while the ever-ballooning national debt is an obvious telltale sign of how out of control we've been, we'd be better off looking inward at our own middle-class financial deficiencies to prove we're still at the circus. As in, the median income of the middle class in 2016 was about the same as it was in 2000. You know what didn't stay the same over that time period? Insurance premiums, petroleum prices, administrative fees, medication costs, education costs, travel costs, entertainment costs, utility costs, food, software, hardware, housing. Throw in corporate greed, corporate debt, political apathy, lobbyists, inflation, deflation, stagflation, bond fluctuations, quantitative easing, trade wars, tariffs, austerity measures, and of course the globalization that now ties all nations together, and you can color me skeptical the Brookings revelation is good news. Too many of our own middle class don't have nearly enough saved for retirement, and WAY too many are living paycheck to paycheck now. Both facts are true of the lower half of the middle class, and they are both fast becoming an issue for the upper half as well. The United States morality is ill-equipped to get us through a major economic storm, and now half the world has joined us? We have zero clue how to shine a solid morality their way as example.

"Shiiiiiit."

But because they are here with us now, they might as well know it will be the simplest of life's needs that threaten our very existence globally. The ones we overlook or take for granted will become our own worst enemy. Basic necessities are as common as a cold, and in the original *War of the Worlds*, it was the common cold that finally killed the aliens. Those tripods were well on their way to domination, but they didn't plan for that little unalloyed virus. They paid the price. So will the world-dominating conspicuous consumers who overlook basic needs.

"Well, any ideas? And please don't tell me to be patient again, Kafka!"

And why can't I?

"Because I want answers now!"

What you want is to skip the hard work and be handed an EASY answer.

"Is that so wrong of me?"

Not only is it NOT wrong, it is human nature.

"So, you're not mad at me?"

I'll answer your question with another: Which is more comfortable, sparring with me as you have, or daring to spar with yourself had I never showed up?

"Definitely with you."

But are you really sparring with me, or have you only really been sparring with yourself?

"Whoa. *A riddle wrapped in a mystery rolled inside an enigma.*"

Ah, yes, Churchill. A Hanged Man if there ever was one. Now how can I be mad at you when you're firing off doozies like that one?

"You...can't be?"

A couch. Alone time. A good book. They are what Prospering Today looks like. You have sought to expand your mind, and it's impossible to be upset with you for such bravery.

"Thanks and all, but still, you've posed some nasty Everest-sized issues to climb."

Mountainous issues cannot be conquered with reflex action, because it was the whole world acting on reflex that created such mountainous issues in the first place.

"I mean—this paradox stuff is a real mother-effer!"

Ha! Human nature is the real motherfucker. The many sides of human nature. The id, the ego, the superego. Not to be outdone, of course, by an even bigger paradox, Nature versus Nurture.

"This is a new Discovery Channel show?"

Probably, but it wasn't where I was going.

"I'm a little afraid of where you might be going."

Only a little?

Are we hard-wired to destroy ourselves (Nature), or can we survive by adapting to our environment through shared experience (Nurture)? There are the obvious red flags that support our predilection for self-destruction: nuclear weapons, climate negligence, mass anesthetizing on narcotics, to name a few, but what about the not-so-obvious red flags?

"Crap. Fine, I know you want me to ask. Such as?"

Such as Barack Obama back-patting himself at the podium for a solid ten minutes while a crowd throbbing with jubilation cheered Bin Laden's assassination. So thirsty for blood we are. Such as capital punishment, the sanctioned killing of our own kind in the name of vengeance. Such as the mammoth incarceration of addicts and the mentally insolvent. Such as the warped mentality it takes to convince ourselves that illegally detaining masses of people in the name of border protection is at all okay. This speaks to immigration and enemies of the state alike, as we have clearly learned no lesson since we confined over a hundred thousand Japanese Americans in internment camps during World War II.

"Egad, man! Tell me the Nurture category looks better."

It does, but not by much. Plenty of us are still pioneers and innovators, but the United States does not lead the world like we think we do. Silicon Valley boasts craploads of annual inventions (we're awesome there), but the United States lags in comparison to the top countries, where a percentage of economic output is devoted to research and development investment. We also lag with respect to scientific and engineering researchers per capita. The most industrious nation on earth should not be lagging behind any country; we should be so far ahead that it would appear as if we were lapping fools in a footrace. Can you guess in which category we of course lap other countries?

"Military spending."

Look at you! Yet, with the percentage of violent war-related deaths decreasing as overall world population increases, are we not living in the most peaceful time in history? And the trend is more peace, not less. Our annual infrastructure expenditures as a percentage of GDP are woeful, our commitment to renewable energy sources by 2030 currently stands at about sixty-five cities. That's nice and all, but the United States has over nineteen thousand cities. And we've already covered where we sit in terms of education.

"Well, which is more important? Please say Nurture."

Nature. I'm a vastly bigger believer in Nature than in Nurture. Shared experience, parental guidance, and societal structure are all important, no doubt, but they are no match for DNA. At some point, it's all going to come out in the wash. Then again, how you choose to embrace your inner algorithm dedicated to free will and let it shine is entirely up to you.

Born with a certain sexual preference that is counter to the norm? No amount of religious boot camp scrubbing is going to quell the urges, so maybe let the flag fly and enjoy yourself if you live in a developed country and won't be persecuted for your predilections. Lack any shred of musical talent but are determined to lead a band? You absolutely can, though prepare to devote countless more hours to the craft than anyone innately more musically talented. Would Genghis Khan have been a foot soldier instead of founder of the Mongol Empire had he not been married off at age nine and later enslaved by his father's former allies? Maybe. But now we're touching on destiny.

"Speaking of destiny, are you saying we are destined to destroy ourselves?"

Way to sneak that question in!

"Well, are we?"

That depends on which definition of *destroy* you gravitate toward. Destroy: *To utterly defeat.* Destroy: *To put an end to the existence of something.* Destroy: *To ruin emotionally or spiritually.* Perhaps our destiny is not to utterly defeat ourselves and end our own existence. Perhaps we only ruin ourselves spiritually and emotionally until we are no longer recognizable.

"Perhaps these concepts are not mutually exclusive, and we will ultimately find our way and thrive as a species well into the future."

Ah, yes, it is always my favorite part of the story when the pupil becomes the teacher. Perhaps you are ready to hang from your own branch soon, my friends.

"That really is some Yoda shit right there. But don't you dare smiley face me again!"

The first few years after leaving the Sunset Marquis job, I lived a languished existence, feeling like I was still stuck in life's version of neutral. My career languished, my relationships languished, and therefore I chose to see the analyst mentioned earlier. Together we asked: Why is Pfeffer hesitating to propel forward? Where are all the fruits of Pfeffer's labor by now? What, pray tell, is Pfeffer not seeing about himself that is holding him back? It was here I learned about suffering and my pop culture impressionability and my will to win and my calculating nature and my inner beasts and my thirst for power and my sacrifices at my own expense and my partiality toward introversion. It is also where I learned I am a slow learner.

"You're about to tell me why this is a positive."

See that, Hanged Man? You are ever so close.

One of the cardinal mistakes during a job interview when asked to name your strengths is to answer that you are a "quick study"; your potential employer may be concerned they will have to ardently groom you. Such a heavy load having to groom someone is these days. 😊

"Knock it off already!"

But can we all really be such adroit learners? Such "quick studies"? I know I am not. I require time and repetitions and conditioning and time.

"You said time twice."

Purposefully. After all, the world is mad with speed now and we should all consider slowing down when we can, lest we overrun—ruin—ourselves spiritually and emotionally. Prosper Today first, and the Perpetuating Tomorrow is all but guaranteed to follow.

"You know, that mantra of yours is a bit Star Trek-ish. *Live long and prosper* and all."

You think I'm going to rebut that?

"I guess it WAS a good show."

It was a cultural phenomenon that sparked an interest in the cosmos.

"Okay, so it was a DAMN good show."

Pop culture at its finest.

"But Captain Kirk and crew engaged with their enemies, and you promised me the sweet taste of victory. When do we get to kick some ass like Churchill did?!"

Churchill may have led Great Britain to victory during World War II, but he also sanctioned human rights abuses attempting to thwart anti-imperialist movements seeking independence from one very repressive empire.

"Of courssse he did."

If only he had Spock to balance him out and keep him from making crazy-poor decisions, like Captain Kirk did, right?

"Oh, sure. If only."

Truly, I get that you are excited for a battle, but please, do not be so concerned with the slaying of all these dragons. All in good time. Take leave of your post first, soldier, I implore you.

For now, continue decompressing on a couch somewhere by yourself with a glass of something strong and a good book (this book will do nicely). Or perhaps you need a break from all this elliptical thought and a movie is on the agenda later tonight? Seriously, I take zero offense if another form of reflection is needed. In fact, might I recommend *Glengarry Glen Ross* for your viewing pleasure? Frank Castle gives it two big thumbs way up!

CHAPTER SIX

A LIKABLE WHITE MALE

"Are you kidding with this chapter title, or what?"

Okay, look. I could just as easily remove this entire chapter and still feel confident the book will have made all the points I aimed to cover. I could pull it, you would never know it once existed, and I could save myself the potential ridicule it will garner if I misstep. But to do so would be cowardly, and as you yourself said, you don't take me for a milksop.

"Not at this point I don't."

Milksop—another outdated word that can easily be construed as a slur—and as also discussed, words do matter. Greatly. So does admitting that the overtly reformist moments already covered have me feeling a twinge awkward. The, making sure I mention all sexes and genders to include everyone, type moments. Because even though I wholeheartedly believe in every word written and believe in leaving them in, Hanged Man does not hold back with his friends. And well, my friends, these moments have me wondering if they hold less weight because I am a white male and it appears I'm only putting them in the book to soften that fact.

You know what else? It is not lost on me that up until now, all the major quotations I have referenced in this book have been made by white males. Those authors, historians, and poets are who I am most comfortable with, and who I aspire to be like as a writer, and I don't want to apologize for that. I won't apologize for being a white male or for feeling most comfortable with the revered words of other white males, and you wouldn't respect me if I did. But know this: I, along with countless other aging white men, recognize how imperative it is we forgo our advantaged status. And not in due time, mind you, but forgo this status immediately.

I have ZERO idea what it feels like to be a nonwhite, nonmale person in this world. But I too often forget that. I too often convince myself that I'm a liberal with a ton of diverse acquaintances who already knows better, so whatever slur, whatever joke, whatever biased remark I'm making at another's expense is okay by default. It's not. And while I used to get defensive about being targeted as a white male who can't make these remarks while others can, I am clear as day now that they are especially harmful coming from a white male, and that I, along with others like me, can contribute best by working tirelessly to knock it the fuck off.

White men have but one job now. One job, in two parts. The first part is to stop believing for even one second that we could ever put ourselves in anyone else's skin, because white men will all forever have ZERO idea who it is to be a nonwhite, nonmale person in this world. The second part of our job now is to recognize the quite obvious and enormous disparities between white men and everyone else and to start bridging that gap by whatever means necessary.

Until I was fourteen, I grew up a forty-five-minute drive north of New York City in the county of Westchester, in a little division of the township of Harrison called Purchase. As of the last census in 2010, Purchase had about six thousand five hundred inhabitants, and probably fewer when I grew up there. It is 78 percent white, 8 percent Asian, and 7 percent black, with other races making up the rest. I attended Harrison High School for one year, and it has less than a 3 percent black demographic. Most of the people I knew were either Jewish, Irish, or Italian, and the Italian and Irish kids vastly outnumbered every other ethnicity and race.

I moved away to Denver between my freshman and sophomore years of high school. Oh yes…Denver, Colorado. Talk about culture shock. I went from attending a public high school with a few hundred students in a close-knit Italian community to attending a public high school with a little over three thousand five hundred students. Then again, was it such a culture shock? The school is 70 percent white, and the percentage of black students is 2 percent.

Having lived in New York and then Colorado, I knew enough at seventeen to want to try something in between for my college experience, so I landed at Indiana University.

"That was a big jump in diversity?"

Not fucking remotely. The student body is currently seventy-eight percent white. And as mentioned in the previous chapter, I joined a fraternity my freshman year, which was comprised almost entirely of other white Jewish kids. Nearly my full freshman year was spent pledging this fraternity, partying with other white members of the Greek system, and avoiding any sense of social responsibility whatsoever. I even moved out of my university dorm, away from whatever traces of diversity campus life provided, and into the fraternity house in the second semester so I could get closer to the party scene, further avoiding any social responsibility. Six weeks into my sophomore year everything changed.

"I'm smelling a scandal."

Scandal? That might be overselling it a bit. You know what? Fuck it. What happened was definitely *morally wrong and caused a fair amount of public outrage.*

The Scavenger Hunt. I remember mine being rollicking good fun when I was a pledge. Thirty-five of us were running all over campus and all over town collecting, bartering, and pleading our way into assembling the items on our list. Then we all met back at the fraternity house and shared our war stories over cases of cheap canned beer. This was not the experience the following pledge class had.

However, before we continue down this path, please bear this in mind—pledge activities were very common, like two to three per week common. So, when I tell you that I had no idea what was on the list given to the pledges until the shit hit the fan the following morning, you can believe me or not believe me, but it's the truth. Still, if you're bent on faulting me for something, you could ask me this question: "Okay, Pfeffer, had you known about what was happening while it was happening, would you have spoken up or even made an effort to stop it?"

No. I don't believe at that point in my life I would have been strong enough to speak up. But I'm strong enough now to admit I once belonged to an organization that let this happen.

The Scavenger Hunt list the freshman pledge class was given had a bigoted preamble atop the list. I don't recall the exact words, but it said something abhorrently derogatory about African Americans. More, the contents of the list itself were offensive to a host of other nonwhite, nonmale groups. And if this all wasn't bad enough, the pledges were further instructed to steal the fraternity letters off an abandoned fraternity house that had been predominantly African American when it was functioning. The few whose task it was to steal those letters were caught by the local police, the police found the scavenger hunt list on the pledges, and then the police turned that list over to the university. All hell broke loose after that.

I'm not sure how to even properly summarize what the remainder of my sophomore year was like. For most students, it was probably like any other year, unceremoniously attending college and opening their eyes wider to stupid shit organized groups allow to happen, like, say, a racially motivated scavenger hunt. But for remaining members of our fraternity, 1997 (and subsequently 1998) were endless internal debates about what we were all going to do, countless school newspaper/local media/even some national media attention, having our charter suspended by our own national fraternity, being kicked out of the Greek system, bomb threats, hiring a sheriff to sit on our front lawn for weeks, town hall–style tongue lashings, racial sensitivity training, waves of anti-Semitism, and ultimately, anger. That's what I really remember from that year. The anger that bubbled up inside of me.

As I sat through racial sensitivity training classes (as agreed upon with the university if we wanted an opportunity to be allowed back in the Greek system), as I read sensationalized story after story in the student newspaper, as I took on more of a leadership role internally to keep our fraternity going while other members abandoned ship, as I helped coordinate a joint party with black student leaders and donated proceeds to their causes, and as I lost out on what I believed was my right to a "normal" college experience filled with intramural sports and sanctioned fraternity parties and sanctioned sorority events to better my odds of hooking up and so, so, so, so, so, so much white privilege—it was the anger I remember most.

Of course, so many decades of forward social movement later, I try not to be too hard on myself about all the misappropriated anger on my part. After all, this experience was just the start of opening my eyes as to what a louse of a white male I was, as well as learning that the combination of me being white and male is an automatic (and understandable) offense to many. More, this experience was also just the start of comprehending partisan machinations of race and power after the fallout of an incident like the Scavenger Hunt. I received a great education watching that fallout ooze into the respective communal canals of all involved.

"As in, how all races and genders and ethnicities involved handled the fallout?"

Exactly like that.

"And?"

Let's just say we all could have done better. The town and university included.

"Well, you said yourself there have been decades of forward social movement since your time in college, so, maybe we're getting better at it now?"

What we've gotten better at is lying to ourselves that we're REALLY talking about it.

"Turn on the TV! It's ALL anyone seems to talk about."

Funny you should mention television.

It was sometime in the second semester of my junior year that I was absolutely convinced I'd be moving to Los Angeles to join the entertainment industry not long after graduation. And though this consciousness did little but aid my already poor business school grades, my move to Hollywood is exactly what happened the summer after receiving my diploma. It was a thrilling time in my life. A new chapter, a chance to spread wings, a step into the industry I had been dreaming about. And whereas so many of my experiences in Tinseltown were positive, let me also tell you here and now that the racial inaptness during my time at Indiana University may have been one thing, but it was pittance compared to what I was about to encounter in Hollywood. Also...yeah...triple that with regard to chauvinism.

All the stories you hear—all the inequality, all the favoritism, all the sexism, prejudices, disproportions, coverups, grotesque behavior, dastardly deeds, and overall inculcation that white male dominance is the most important doctrine—I'm here to tell you they're all true. Even now. Even as female and nonwhite protagonists are populating our television screens, and as nonwhite and non-American content is gaining steam, and as pay is equalizing, and as private hotel room meetings are going by the wayside, and as the Harvey Weinsteins of the world are being dethroned, it's still beyond disproportionately white and male to the trained eye, and that's exactly how those in power would rather it be kept. Don't expect me to name names (this isn't a rooting out of Communists), and you can tell me I'm off base as the atmosphere changes (I'm not), because the white male still rules all in Hollywood, and this is not going to change any time soon. Not without a monumental effort from white males themselves.

"But you just proved it IS being addressed."

Addressing something in an isolated comfort zone is not the same as REALLY addressing something outside of said comfort zone. Cognitive scientist Noam Chomsky (yep, another white guy reference) once presciently said, "the smart way to keep people passive and obedient is to strictly limit the spectrum of acceptable opinion but allow very lively debate in that spectrum."

You already know my writing partner and I worked on the all-white *Fantastic Four* sequel. The one BEFORE a black Johnny Storm ignited an alt-right fanboy fervor online. The one where Jessica Alba was the closest to depicting diversity in the top-billed cast. The one where Kerry Washington played the blind love interest to The Thing...a metaphorical role about race that badly missed the mark. The one where Andre Braugher played military man General Hager, following in the footsteps of so many black actors relegated to secondary onscreen roles of military, law enforcement, scientist, or legal team. The one where the Silver Surfer was played by a white actor onscreen yet voiced by a black actor (Laurence Fishburne).

I mentioned earlier that the director of these two *Fantastic Four* installments was Tim Story, who is black, and that my writing partner and I worked intimately for a long time with Tim's development executive, who is also black. It was this development executive who ever-so-patiently remolded our *Robin Hood* script into something readable, and who ever-so-patiently educated me on the would-be behaviors of our nonwhite characters as I fumbled through the first attempts. It was this development exec who opened my eyes to the holiday and overall importance of Juneteenth, an annual festival held on June 19 to commemorate the emancipation of slavery in Texas, and ultimately the entire Union. I never learned that in any school. I owe this man a great debt of gratitude for his tireless tutoring. We may not have won the writing job or made a dime during our time on this project, but I was paid handsomely in edification.

Next came my job at the bar, which was procured by another friend (the manager at the hotel) who is black. I mention him because he's an interesting guy who has also taught me a great deal. Particularly, that he and his wife, who are Jamaican, abhor being labeled African Americans. More edification.

Shortly after I landed the bar gig, Barack Obama was elected president. Which, as a maturing liberal was a great boost to my morale at the end of 2008, and an even greater moment when he took office on January 20, 2009. But the subsequent eight years of his figure in the White House were filled with such limited generalizations about race in this country that I was most dismayed with how little progress was being made on the matter, even as a black person filled the most powerful position on earth. Chomsky's pronouncement is all too often what those eight years felt like: we were debating about race in a lively manner, sure, but we were doing so in a limited spectrum, and we were doing so to maintain a decorum that no longer needs maintaining the way we maintain it.

Then came August 26, 2016.

If you were to Google "August 26, 2016," the first link brings you to a calendar, but the second link whisks you to the top ten things that happened on this day according to *The Week* magazine. Not one of the ten unremarkable pieces of news listed covers what I am referring to. The same can be said of *The Week*'s top ten news list for August 27. But on August 28, 2016, it hit number nine on the list.

It read, 49ers COLIN KAEPERNICK RAISES CONTROVERSY BY REFUSING TO STAND FOR THE NATIONAL ANTHEM. He had already sat twice for the anthem on August 14 and again on August 20, but he was not in uniform for either of those games, and these were meaningless preseason games to begin with, so it had gone unnoticed. He was officially in uniform on August 26 for the last preseason game, and he finally addressed his actions on August 28, 2016: "People don't realize what's really going on in this country. There are a lot of things going on that are unjust. People aren't being held accountable for. And that's something that needs to change. That's something that this country stands for—freedom, liberty, and justice for all. And it's not happening for all right now."

More...

"These aren't new situations. This isn't new ground. There are things that have gone on in this country for years and years and have never been addressed, and they need to be."

A twelve-, nineteen-, twenty-five-, or maybe even thirty-year-old me would have staunchly admonished his actions. My arguments would have been foolishly similar to others': disrespect for the military, shut up and play the game, you're not even a prominent enough player to lead these protests, to name a few.

"But the thirty-seven-year-old, Pfeffer?"

The thirty-seven-year-old Pfeffer was an immediate supporter of Colin Kaepernick, and I'm an even bigger one today. I may be ambivalent about a great many violators of societal rules who shed necessary light via their actions (Edward Snowden and Chelsea Manning come to mind), but Colin Kaepernick is unmistakably a hero of mine. And as a martyr who is currently unemployed by a league that should be embracing him instead of imprudently shunning him, AND as a schismatic symbol of a branding giant like Nike, he's the perfect iconoclastic image for the new age of civil rights. Moreover, with enough support, the revolution he sparked will prove to be on the right side of history, and you know how I feel about revolutions.

Time will tell if the outward growth of his actions can continue reverberating the way Rosa Parks's refusal to sit in the back of the bus did, but I (and many others) would not be out of line to compare the two, and I'm rooting like hell that a figure the magnitude of Dr. Martin Luther King Jr. will emerge soon to beat the drums of Kaepernick's cause until they are an unavoidable uproar in everyone's ears. Know this—my reverence for Kaepernick's actions did not arise without a good many instances and good many people shedding light in my direction along my life's path. Allow me to help continue shedding more.

Men and women of color are absolutely being brutalized and, in all too many instances, being murdered by police enforcement. And we keep trying to pretend this is not really happening, and we keep letting the officers in question and ultimately ourselves off the hook. There is no other way to describe the killing of unarmed citizens but as *murder*, and there is no other reason for decades of abuse since the first civil rights movement other than racism. Racism…

The belief that all members of each race possess characteristics or abilities specific to that race, especially so as to distinguish it as inferior or superior to another race or races.

Let's dissect this, because this definition may be where we keep tripping ourselves up as a collective. It should not be that a Gordian knot of racial interpretation limits our next steps toward equality, but it too often feels like this has happened. Discrimination, prejudice, and antagonism are NOT necessarily racism UNTIL they are directed against someone of a different race BASED ON THE BELIEF THAT ONE'S OWN RACE IS SUPERIOR.

We all must remember that last part about superiority (and inversely, inferiority), because we are watering down the message of racism now, and we are quick to label everything as racism when true racism is a category unto itself. This is what all those racial sensitivity classes back at Indiana University taught me. We all have prejudices, we all discriminate for countless reasons, and we can all find ourselves in the position to antagonize other humans who don't mirror ourselves, but are these tendencies always based in a belief of racial superiority?

"No, they really aren't."

True racism looks like profiling followed by unwarranted harassment. Racism looks like systematic incarceration of an outrageous number of citizens of certain groups with sentences that don't match the crimes. Racism looks like the sustained murder (of any degree) of a certain sect of people by another certain sect of people with a superiority complex. Racism looks like withholding resources that would boost the educational opportunities in African American, Native American, Hispanic, Asian, and any nonwhite neighborhoods for that matter.

Moreover, the issues of one race are not their issues alone, they are everyone's issues. Why are we not getting that? Colin Kaepernick gets that. Yet he's vilified because pissing on the American flag is no way to go about bringing attention to a big-assed problem? He's slapping the military in the face? He's using grounds (sports) that are too hallowed to besmirch with political statements? No, I don't think so. These are yet more excuses. More reduction of the subject matter so we can keep letting ourselves off the hook and continue avoiding the larger problem that is not going away anytime soon.

Wake up. Wake the fuck up and stand for something like Colin Kaepernick does. Question your own shoe deal, your money, every other athlete who hides behind insincere mumblings of military support. Especially the white athletes who are nowhere to be found on this issue. Question your status in the community, every politician holding office and clinging to their capital base by walking some bullshit tonal tightrope every day. Question the hell out of your ledger, every bounty hunter, bail bondsman, and privatized prison making a dime off the backs of nonwhite citizens.

Don't tell me I'm naive. Don't tell me I don't know how the world works, and I'd be better off living in the blissful ignorance of conspicuous consumption and weekend prayer to false idols while my brethren burn. I'm forty years old now, not some idealistic kid whose dreams will never be realized. I'm the new breed of aging white male, motherfucker, and there are millions like me just itching to stand up alongside Kaepernick. Secular, liberal, educated, but still loyal to the almighty dollar just like you are. Am I a fucking likable-enough white male for you now?!

"Annnnnnnnnnd, wow. WOW. But in all your racial evangelizing, you kind of forgot how a white male might also be coming across to everyone else, especially the opposite sex."

No, I hadn't forgotten, but your statement just made for a nice transition, thanks.

"You're...welcome?"

"The Wake of Weinstein." This wake is one very large, very important reverberation that has rightly registered around an 11.7 on the chromosomal Richter scale.

"That's kind of an odd number. What's the highest Richter scale measurement?"

There is no limit on the scale. But according to a forum with some knowledgeable participants, a 10.0 quake could rip a continent in half, an 11.0 is likened to something impacting the planet with such force that the energy released would flood the entire surface with boiling lava, and a 12.0 conjures enough oomph that not even gravity is strong enough to keep the planet from splitting in two. That's where we're at. The recent SCOTUS hearings and Harvey Weinstein ignominy have set off reverberations that have and will continue to rumble with enough power that not even gravity can keep in place what once existed. Nor should it. Nor is it okay that white men alone be making any decisions on anyone's future any more.

"Whew! Tall order, even in this day and age. So, what comes next?"

What comes next is what comes first. One job in two parts. White males no longer pretending they could possibly share any inkling what it's like to be anyone other than them, and those same white males relinquishing all their power without a fight.

"How long should I hold my breath?"

How much lung capacity do you have?

"Riiiiiight. Also, I have to say I'm not crazy about insinuating white men have all the power to begin with. It diminishes everyone else's power they all have, even if they don't realize they hold more power than they know."

Could it even be possible for you to have given a better Hanged Man response than that one?

"I'm officially going to say no, it could not be possible."

Alice Walker said, "The most common way people give up their power is by thinking they don't have any."

"Exactly. It is not enough for white men alone to relinquish all their power, because all others already hold power they themselves should never be relinquishing."

You're starting to sound like me.

"I might need some time to consider if I like that or not."

Take all the time you need.

"Alice Walker, huh? There goes your streak of quoting only white men."

Good.

CHAPTER SEVEN

A TECHNOLOGICALLY CAPABLE LUDDITE

I'M FIFTEEN, I'VE made the move to Denver already, I'm out to dinner one night with my new best friend and his family, and he proclaims that it won't be long until we're all microchipped and our brains hooked up permanently to computers. (Yes, we actually talked like this at fifteen years old, and yes, this was the conversation being held over spareribs and wonton soup.) I scoffed and disagreed, and then further proclaimed that I never wanted to use a computer as part of my daily life if I could help it. Then he called me a Luddite. And because I had no idea what the hell a Luddite was, he cordially explained it was a label for someone who shunned technology completely. Ever eager to play the role of contrarian, I liked the sound of that and ran my mouth to all in attendance about how I was going to shun technology for as long as possible! Then I slept over his house that night and we logged into his AOL dialup account, where I proceeded to play the game of *Risk* online until the sun came up. The year was 1994, and in case you hadn't noticed, we were dope as fuck.

Desktops, laptops, tablets, smartphones, yadda yadda—you got me, I have 'em all. I haven't been microchipped yet, and my brain hasn't been hooked into a central data center (at least I don't think it has, or I don't think we're living in the Matrix, or I don't think existence is a hologram projected through a wormhole onto a neutron star, but I've been wrong before). Now it's twenty-five years after my great Chinese Restaurant Proclamation, and do you think I'm a lackey to the technological core four like pretty much everyone else? You bet your ass I am. Because though I may have destroyed cotton and wool milling machinery across England in the very early 1800s as the original Luddites did, here and now in the United States, I own imprudent amounts of technological hardware and utilize indiscreet amounts of technological software. Pride can be a loathsome creature. Pride is one of the original seven deadly sins. But what can I say? I pride myself on efficiency, and all this technology makes me feel quite efficient.

GAFA: Google, Apple, Facebook, Amazon. The Four Horsemen of the Infocalypse. Well, to be fair, when someone refers to the Four Horsemen of the Infocalypse, they are referring to any number of ethereal cybercriminals, not GAFA, but I think we're missing a great meta opportunity here, so help me redirect the narrative, if you will.

"Except I love all those companies. Even own some stock."

Hmm.

"Uh-oh."

Two years before my Luddite-infused wonton soup (twenty-seven years ago for those counting), another of my favorite films was released. Redford! Poitier! Kingsley! Strathairn!

"No clue here."

Mary McDonnell, Dan Aykroyd, Timothy Busfield, Stephen Tobolowsky, River Phoenix!

"Not at all helping me figure it out any faster."

SNEAKERS. A crack security team is blackmailed by government agents into recovering a device capable of decrypting the world's invulnerable systems, but no one is really who they say they are, and soon our heroes are embroiled in a dangerous game of cat and mouse.

"Sounds pretty good. And?"

And Ben Kingsley seriously delivers as rogue villain Cosmo. Like, seriously delivers.

COSMO: *The world isn't run by weapons anymore, or energy, or money. It's run by little ones and zeroes, little bits of data. It's all just electrons.*

This was 1992, mind you. Merely two years after the World Wide Web went mainstream.

COSMO: *There's a war out there, old friend. A world war. And it's not about who's got the most bullets. It's about who controls the information. What we see and hear, how we work, what we think... it's all about the information!*

Add Netflix to the acronym GAFA and you create a new acronym recently popularized in our zeitgeist, FAANG. For a moment in May 2018, Netflix was briefly worth more than Disney, the premiere media company of the world, with a market cap well north of $100 billion. Disney was founded in 1923 and currently owns the likes of ABC Television, ESPN Network, Pixar, Lucasfilm, Marvel Entertainment, and soon 20th Century Fox assets and a 39 percent stake in Sky TV. Oh, and Disney also owns and operates six massive resorts and employs two hundred thousand worldwide. Netflix was founded in 1997, has fifty-four hundred employees, owns DVD.com, ABQ Studios, and something called Millarworld. But what do they really have? They have a proprietary algorithm that tracks the user information of their 140 million subscribers down to a fucking tee. They have the little ones and zeroes. The little bits of data. They have the information.

Google has the information. Apple has the information. Amazon has the information. And Facebook? Facebook not only has the information, but between the main company and its ownership of Instagram and WhatsApp, it is also the clear world leader of social media with a monthly user base north of 2.3 billion. Google+ has 540 million users (though the consumer version is shutting down soon). YouTube (owned by Google) has nearly 2 billion users of varying degree. Amazon delved in with Spark, but it ain't exactly noteworthy yet. Apple doesn't employ social media, though it is kind enough to offer some very fun emojis for all.

"Well, how many users does Twitter have?"

Three hundred thirty-six million. LinkedIn claims around 500 million. Pinterest is around 200 million. Tumblr has over 400 million blog accounts, and Snapchat also garners around 400 million daily users. Social media up the ying-yang.

Cat videos. Enough pictures of ourselves and family and friends and food that countless coders and servers will forever be needed to safeguard them in the cloud for eternity. Pithy comedic and dramatic thought bubbles encapsulated in 140-character-long Tweets. Dog videos. Direct messaging and shared secrets between friends, enemies, and lovers. Unbesmirched peer reviews of eateries, dwellings, jobs, and establishments. Bird videos. Access to all facets of world news, including live on-the-ground-as-it's-happening updates. Horse videos. Travel navigation capability. Whale videos. Deliveries. Goat videos. Erotica. Duck videos. Monkey videos. Giraffe videos. Komodo dragon videos! There is a lot to like about social media, indeed.

"Oh, here it comes."

Yes, comrades, here is comes.

Let's start with the paralysis of analysis. To borrow a term often used in the world of real estate investing, the constant checking in, or logging in, has been known to cause much anxiety, which can then lead to much pause in our follow-up actions as a result of fear. Namely, fear of missing out, so we don't then log out. Fear of spending too much time living online, which makes us miss out on the outside world. And, perhaps worst of all, fear of offending anybody, as our avatars are expected to be perfect little extensions of ourselves. Thusly, we are paralyzed by our own overanalyzing of the social media game, and we end up as frightened, smiling wallflowers afraid to ask anyone to dance.

Next comes public shaming. Or, naming and shaming. The pitchforked mob will have their blood, and they are super adept at banding together and outing their target. And once this target has been brought before the tribunal, well, we took time out of our busy days to be here and all, so a witch must burn! Phone numbers, home addresses, personal information—all must be revealed so our target has nowhere to run, nowhere to hide. All forms of scarlet letter shall be branded on our target so that all can identify them, and then all can admonish them for their actions until the end of time itself. Gross.

The recruitment of our loved ones is also happening. Unlike the irrational fear that pedophilic predators are just waiting in every park across the land to snatch your child, it's way more likely someone is going to get them online if they're going to get them. And not necessarily pedophiles. There are plenty of other scary predators acting as false friends to children.

"Like conmen or cult members or even ISIS."

You know what? Yeah, like conmen, cult members, or even ISIS. I abhor fear mongering more than anyone, so I'm not trying to beat the drums too hard here, but subversive recruitment to all types of nefarious shit lurks in the halls of social media, so don't let your guard down out there.

Speaking of, social media offers the perfect pulpit to monger fear, and it's proven disgraceful. Followed closely by fake news, doctored videos, phishing scams, hacking threats, and—not to be outdone—the constant annoyance of troubleshooting innumerable technical glitches. The young seem not to be bothered by the troubleshooting (as they were born into it), but there are those of us who remember what it was like prior to spending our lives fixing bugs and waiting for the feed to catch up to itself. It bothers me most because I know there are so many Millennials and Centennials who could fix in minutes the issues that sometimes cost me hours, and the competitor in me deplores being slow.

"You sound old again."

My aching back already tells me I'm old! Where was I? Right… still, nothing compares to the biggest and darkest issue with social media. Drum roll, please! No? Fuck, whatever.

"Privacy."

I know…wasn't hard to see where I was going there.

"Nope."

Ah, but do you know where I'll be bringing us next?

"Applebee's?"

They do have some of the better mozzarella sticks in the business, but no, not Applebee's.

Most, if not all, of the social media darkness already mentioned can be avoided by heavy doses of education about the malfeasances or extremely limited or no partaking. But even a nonuser like me can't outrun the privacy issue. For starters, I used to partake a little (still do), which means my information is already out there and Cambridge Analytica and so many other consulting and data mining firms like it already know everything about me. And even if you are the strictest social media vegan, unless you are so purposefully hermetic, so off the grid that you most likely don't have a social security number, then they've got you too. And that is fucking scary. It's scary because those who have such understanding of analytics compared to the rest of us could squash us like bugs with that knowledge. And it's scary because it's the governments of the world that will ultimately end up with ALL the information no matter what FAANG promises.

But the scariest part about losing our privacy? Privacy is a human right, and a violated human right is a death knell.

Human rights have been trampled since the time there ever were humans, so the oppressive boot on our collective neck is nothing new, but this level of grand-scale agreement to willingly hand over a human right is unprecedented. Exactly, we daily sign unread agreements relinquishing this right, and it was designed this way purposefully from the get-go, so the duplicity is even more staggering. Our technology addictions are a Faustian deal if there ever was one, and the devil now has way more than just our personal information—it has our signed consent to access our privacy.

The United Nations recognizes thirty human rights, and the right to privacy in the digital age falls under United Nations Resolution 68/167: "That no one shall be subjected to arbitrary or unlawful interference with his or her privacy, family, home or correspondence, nor to unlawful attacks on his or her honor and reputation."

When a basic human right is threatened like this, it is imperative that we understand that ANYONE who manipulates their agenda to impose that threat does not have an appropriate regard for human life. Not every villain wears the uniform of a Nazi or other nefarious coat of armor. Some come in the form of innocuous-looking nerds.

"Yikes. Maybe a little judgmental?"

Oh, how fantastically ironic it is that we hate to be judged nowadays. Never mind that I told you my jury duty anecdote or even suggested "judge me as you will" for invoking my niece in a discussion about the Lord's existence, right? Our entire society is based on judgment of our actions; rest assured, you yourself will stand before the Black Robed if the system deems you have fucked up royally enough. One of our three imperative branches of government (judicial) is rife with judgment. Hell, some of our most popular reality shows rely on the snarky charisma of judges to remain atop the television ratings. To pass no judgment is to make no observation of the world. And you want to tell me judging the technological autocrats who hold dominion over our privacy isn't nice? Nice went out the window when a few of the meek got tired of being invisible to whoever they hoped noticed them, gamed the system, and now everyone else has to live "publicly," even if other nerds such as myself would rather not. Cosmo from *Sneakers* was a lovable college dork with a big utopian dream in the beginning of the movie, but he sure didn't end up that way.

"Maybe Zuckerberg won't ever have Cosmo's nefarious intentions."

Maybe not yet, but plenty of the same issues regarding information have been brought to his attention, and still he presses on. And he and those pilfering our information who understand analytics best are getting dangerously close to a full-on violation.

"Still, I kind of like when Google analyzes my emails for keywords and then uses it to sell me stuff. As long as I'm consuming conspicuously and all, might as well make it easy."

And therein lies our dilemma. On the one hand we may want our technological overlords to know us better than we know ourselves, constantly directing us toward better decision making. But on the other hand, the shitty inevitable is currently part of the deal too—those gathering our personal information constantly needing to gather even more for a better company market value, followed by ceaselessly promoting the message they are doing YOU the favor by harboring your info, and then naturally their own overlords (regulatory institutions) confiscating all our gathered personal information when it suits them. But what's REALLY happening above all? Our privacy gets chipped away just a little bit extra each time we agree to make it easier on tech companies to sell us stuff. Well, privacy is going to be obsolete if we continue down this path, privacy is a human right, and anyone who knowingly violates a human right does not have a regard for human life. Regard. For. Human. Life.

"Perpetuate Tomorrow?"

[Robust head bobbing]

When push comes to shove, and human beings get condensed into ones and zeroes, into numbers, they are no longer human. No humble tech guru, no analytics consulting firm, and certainly no government should have the power to virtually tattoo numbers onto humans the way Nazis literally tattooed numbers onto humans.

"It's just…this feels like a really big leap we're making from cat videos."

Is it now? At least FAANG is the face of a democratic Western civilization. You can't necessarily say the same about BAT.

"There's another acronym?!?!"

Baidu, Alibaba, Tencent.

China. The People's Republic of China. Anyone who thinks they are communist only in name now might also like to see this big, beautiful bridge in Brooklyn I have for sale. The party is the only true land owner in China, and the people forever remain property of the state—1.4 billion properties of the state. They now have the world's second largest economy as well.

Baidu is the Google of China. Alibaba is their Amazon. Tencent is Facebook. Actually, Tencent is now worth more than Facebook. BAT doesn't need to be duplicitous about consent to privacy from their users because their user base already belongs to the state. We're all up in arms over here that the NSA and sixteen other national security agencies are constantly trying to cajole FAANG (and our cell phone providers) into handing over personal information, but in China, it's handed over right off the…

"Bat?"

Better you made the pun.

And still, STILL! with all this concern over the threat of too much information getting into the hands of our governments or analytics firms interfering with our elections (as one nefarious example) or aging tech gurus going all "Cosmo" on us, I remain a massive proponent of the overall world shrinking that social media and, really, all forms of technology afford us.

"Massive proponent you say."

Like $30 billion massive.

"That's a pretty specific number you've got yourself there."

It's the current valuation of the sex tech industry is what it is.

"Jesus H. Christ!"

Now who's the blasphemer?

"Still, what exactly are you getting at?"

Sexual androids.

"Ehhhhhh, what's this now?"

Animatronic robots for the purposes of sexual gratification.

"You sneaky little SOB."

Sit this one out if you must, but much like the taxman, they inevitably cometh.

"Wait, was that some sort of sordid pun?"

When the shoe fits and all.

"*Blech!*"

Gag on, but virtual reality pornography, AI-enhanced sexual gaming, and phone apps for finding a nightly hookup only scratch the surface of what is already under our noses. Intimate android companions, android brothels, and, ultimately, full-on human-to-android domestic relationships are the next leap sex tech is about to take. And not fifty years from now. Now, now. All three are here already, they will explode in popularity from this day forward, and whatever Luddites are left could never come close to stopping this ensuing surge of sexualized robots that is primed for a societal explosion.

"I can't quite tell if you're bothered by this."

Not remotely.

"Even as a married man with a family?"

Nuh-huh. In fact, it's because I feel so comfortable in the monogamous commitment I made to my soulmate that I'm emboldened enough by my own vows not to let the proclivities of another disturb my world. Like, say, marriage between a woman and another woman. Or interracial love affairs or love affairs that cross religious and cultural boundaries that neither I nor anyone else should dare have a say in.

"I see what you're doing there. But those are still HUMAN relationships. How does the rise of sexualized robots help us Perpetuate Tomorrow?"

Oh, I am so, so, so, so glad you asked.

I'm just going to put this as bluntly as I can—we decidedly NEED an android sexual revolution to spark the next phase of human advancement.

"[Deafening silence]"

Um, hello? Why so quiet suddenly?

"Six chapters, Pfeffer. Six chapters you've had my head spinning. You led me up, down, sideways, this way and that, and for all six chapters I've wanted to tell you to 'screw off,' but you kept just making so much damn sense! Not this time. You're not going to get me with your elliptical argumentative nonsense on this one. SCREW OFF!"

You know, I expected this from a lot of people, but not from you.

"Oh, come on, that's not fair."

I thought we were getting close.

"We were. We are. But needing an android sexual revolution? Dude, you're asking a lot."

It's not easy being a contrarian, I know. The naysayers can't wait to thump a good nonconformist back down, and we need to stick together.

"What naysayers, exactly?"

Well, for starters, spools of Reddit thread will be spun debating my motivations, and plenty will tear apart my arguments. The trolls will lambaste me for having relied too heavily on Wikipedia and *Forbes* for intel. Someone will find a wonky fact or three and use it as basis to discredit the entire work. I'll be accused of egregiously regurgitating the thoughts of others, and that none of these ideas was original to begin with. Critics will be furious with me for not covering ENOUGH ground: "He left out Syria as well as the precipitous decline in sperm count among European men. Oh, and shark attacks. Also, he mentioned a ton of past presidents but didn't lambaste our sitting one with extreme prejudice, like I would have!" Naysayers galore.

"Don't forget that the liberal publications who cover this book will make it about themselves, like they always do, and the conservative ones will only key in on your love of capitalism and support of certain gun rights."

You see?! You get me.

"Dammit, man. But does it have to be sex robots that save us?"

Yes. I'm afraid it does.

"Well then."

Well then.

"Well then, let's coax the miscreants out from their chambers so that all the land can watch as they hurl their feces at you for daring to question the norm. Hit me with some sex robots!"

Love to, but I'm afraid we're out of time in this chapter.

"Are you freaking serious?"

Next chapter, I promise.

"Swear?"

I swear. Sex robots are coming.

"*Blech!*"

CHAPTER EIGHT
A FIGHTER AND A FLIGHTER

I'd like to turn your attention to Earth herself for a moment. There has been a mixed message in circulation for far too long about the human footprint and its devious infliction upon our dear mother. We give ourselves way too much credit, and we need to keep the damage we exact on the six biological kingdoms in perspective compared to the damage we THINK we are exacting on Mother Earth.

Regardless of all the natural resources we mine, timber we cut, oil we burn, nuclear weapons we test, atmosphere we pepper with debris, landfills we create, Texas-sized plastic masses we form in the ocean, or coral reefs we destroy, Mother Earth is not hurting. Not one bit. She is still as stunning as ever, still clean. How? Because she will cleanse us right off her face like a bothersome pimple if we don't clean up our act for the sake of ourselves, not for her.

Think! There have been five massive ice ages in the four and half billion years she has been around, and there have also been five massive extinction periods over that same four and half billion years, which tells us more of both are coming. Hominid evolution (from chimps into six species of *Homo*) occurred only in the last five to eight million years; we're still sorting through the fossils to pinpoint an exact timeline. And the *Homo sapiens* species, aka humans—the only of the six hominid species that endured the primate evolution, we should note—modern humans have been around for between two hundred and three hundred thousand years. That brings us back to the last ice age, which began roughly two and a half million years ago and lasted until about twelve thousand years ago. Humans survived and even thrived during the last ice age. We are clearly exploring how humans must thrive deep into the future, but one thing is for certain: Mother Earth is absolutely going to survive just fine with or without us.

She's going to produce ample more ice ages and grind tectonic plates and erupt the fuck out of supervolcanoes and reverse the magnetism of her poles and fluctuate gulf streams and unleash violent storms, not giving one granule of a shit that her ice shelves are melting and rising sea levels are swallowing land masses. She'll absorb gargantuan sun flares that royally fuck with every living thing on the planet, and she'll withstand asteroid impacts that release the energy of one hundred trillion tons of TNT like the one that helped kill off the dinosaurs around sixty-six million years ago, not batting an eye while she does so. And unless she's unlucky enough to find herself in the line of fire of some random celestial event we can't even yet fathom, Mother Earth is going to keep on trucking until the sun evolves into a red giant and engulfs her. Five billion years from now.

So please stop worrying about Mother Earth. Please stop entangling her beauty with the fate of our existence. She's going to be just fine either way, but we're not. Which means it is high time we admit to ourselves that human beings are selfish creatures, that selfishness is a major reason why we currently sit atop the world's food chain, and that we need to get WAY more selfish in order to make it long term.

"Way more? Is that even possible?"

PROTAGONIST:

1. *The main figure or one of the most prominent figures in a real situation*
2. *An advocate or champion of a particular cause or idea*

So, here's the thing about every person in this biosphere... every single person...all seven point whatever billion people: all of us, each and every one of us, is the protagonist in our own life's story. Please do not take this lightly. Sit with it for a moment. Let the definitions of the word about who you are and what you believe and why you get up every day wash over you a moment.

Because regardless of sex, creed, color, or origin, you are the hero in your own life. You are the champion of your own particular causes or ideas. Yet at the same time, deep down we know we are all merely pawns in the larger concept of life. And that kind of humbling duality can really fuck with you as a person. As a protagonist. Now honor that duality and choose the path of least resistance. Exactly, maintain the current course and keep owning your place at the top of the world food chain. Our future is at stake here, good people.

We are most likely not going to collectively stop mining for resources, though we should all commit to finding useful alternative energies to apply those resources. We are most likely not going to collectively stop gorging ourselves on the flesh of other species, though we should all commit to finding more economical alternatives to chomp into. We are most likely not going to collectively recycle our waste appropriately, though we should all commit to finding more functional ways of utilizing that waste. And we are most likely not going to collectively stem the tide of climate change by ourselves, so we better consider figuring out how life flourishes after the climate is rendered uninhabitable for human existence.

"Let's hear it already, Pfeffer, how do we do that?"

Fire.

"As in…?"

As in, make like the early humans did and cultivate something as amazing as fire was when they left Africa and spread around the globe. We need to refine an invention as paramount as fire, and we better make sure it goes widespread.

"I thought you said the internet was the most important invention in history."

As fucking if! I said the internet's historical importance was one hundred billion times that of the printing press. Neither of those inventions have anything on fire. Fire is life, and life is in serious jeopardy.

We no longer have kiloyears or millennia or even one millennium. We are down to centuries. Maybe even as little as one century, with the recent climate change estimates and Hothouse Earth on our horizon. Somewhere in the next hundred or so years is our window to locate the key to our ensuing move, or it will officially be over for most, if not all of us.

"One hundred divided by 4.5 billion is…not a lot of time in the grand scheme of things!"

December 17, 1903–July 20, 1969. Less than sixty-six years transpired between the first successful airplane flight in Kitty Hawk, North Carolina, and astronauts landing on the damn moon. In less than a century we leaped from a twelve-second flight 120 feet above the ground with a top speed of 6.8 miles per hour to covering a distance of 238,900 miles and walking on the surface of a celestial body that has no breathable atmosphere. Sixty-six years. Way LESS than a century.

This is really why I am such a massive proponent of technology, and even social media. Deep down, *the most prominent figures in a real situation* rely on their instincts for survival. This is why I suspect the scientific revolution began in 1543, and this is why we have recently (cosmically speaking) been cycling through technological advancements at an incredible rate in comparison to that at the dawn of humankind. I believe our collective sixth sense has been sounding the alarm of our impending doom for quite some time now, and EVERYTHING we do is a response to that alarm. Social media especially. Sure, cat videos, and sure, it's a dangerous cesspool for ISIS, and everyone from nefarious tech nerds to big bad governments who prey on our privacy? Right, those fuckers all need to knock it off. Because do you know what social media really is? It's the communicative filament that will bring humanity together the way we were meant to once we stop with all the fake news and learn how to correctly use this tool the same way our monkey ancestors learned how to use the bones of a wooly mammoth as a chisel.

We are officially in fight-or-flight mode, good people. Self-preservation has kicked the fuck in, and whether we remain on Earth and successfully battle the impending climate shift (fight) or get off this rock and establish colonies throughout space (flight), time is of the essence either way. Ergo, time to get WAY more selfish with our scientific activities, continue breaking eggs in the name of survival omelets, and fucking thrive as we must!

"I mean…"

Yeah, I mean it too. Hold the thought, though, because we've got way more to cover here.

In 1964, Soviet astrophysicist Nikolai Kardashev *proposed a method for measuring the level of civilization's technological advancement based on the level of energy that civilization is able to use for communication.* It is now known as the Kardashev scale:

- Type I civilization: a Planetary civilization
- Type II civilization: a Stellar civilization
- Type III civilization: a Galactic civilization

Planetary civilizations can store all the incoming energy from their parent star. Stellar civilizations can utilize the stored energy of their parent star to spread throughout their galaxy. Galactic civilizations can control energy on the scale of their entire host galaxy.

"Dude, we don't fall under any of these categories."

Nice observation, Sherlock. Renowned theoretical physicist Michio Kaku believes we'll become a Type I civilization in the next couple of centuries, and astrobiologist Carl Sagan (one of our most respected scientists before his untimely death) ascertained we are about a Type 0.7 civilization now. Also, though the scale has since been expanded to include other categories, we'll remain focused on just these three. We can get to Type I when we harness fusion and antimatter. Fusion is *the reaction of combining two hydrogen atoms together to form one helium atom, where during that process some of the mass of the hydrogen is converted into energy.* The process of fusion is what powers the sun and the stars, my friends, and we're closer to achieving this than you might think.

"Sweet! And antimatter?"

Antimatter is the material composed of the antiparticle to the corresponding particles of ordinary matter.

"Uhhhhh."

I know, right? Also, stable antimatter currently does not appear to exist in our universe.

"And we're supposed to harness this stuff?"

According to Kaku and a multitude of other astrophysicists we are, and we're also supposedly closer to achieving this task than you might think.

Type II civilizations are expected to build Dyson spheres (or Dyson swarms), so named after another theoretical physicist, Freeman Dyson. These megastructures are supposed to enclose a parent star completely and capture most, if not all, of its energy output.

"You're telling me we're someday going to build a megastructure that encloses our sun and captures its energy?!"

You're telling me Bitcoin isn't a common "pump and dump" scheme and will someday become the primary currency of the entire world?

"Ha! Wait…so I should sell my Bitcoin?"

Look, I'm not saying any of this is going to happen, and we should further scrutinize the scale itself for claiming to know what all advanced alien life must do to achieve interplanetary communication and travel. As of now, we don't know if there is only one universe or if we are part of a multiverse, we've yet to encounter any true evidence of other intelligent life at all, and most of us can't make heads or tails of the Fermi paradox.

"Yes, of course, the Fermi paradox."

You know of the Fermi paradox?

"Naturally, I do. Why do you think I bought all that Bitcoin?"

Uh-huh. What I'm driving at and why I brought up the scale at all is to show that our highest minds are already understanding the need for pure human avarice. That good kind of true selfishness that ensures the preservation of our human lineage. However, if Dyson spheres aren't getting your acquisitive juices flowing, Type II civilizations could also explore star lifting, where we potentially remove a substantial portion of the sun's matter using a controlled method wherein antimatter could be recycled since it will have been produced as an industrial by-product of this megascale engineering.

"Oh, sure. Naturally."

Um, do you even want to hear about Type III civilizations that will have developed self-replicating robots capable of tapping into supermassive black holes to then extract the energy of a white hole for the vitality needed to keep our Matrioshka Brains whirring?

"Not without mozzarella sticks first, but def gonna sell that Bitcoin thanks to Kardashev!"

Yeaaaaaaaaaaah. Anyway, the current worldwide average for a single human life span is approximately seventy-two years, right? If and when possible, that average human should Prosper Today by finding as much time in their own life to decompress, relax with a glass of something strong on a couch somewhere (obvious Western hemisphere vision), and enjoy the hell out of their seventy years. As discussed, a single human deserves whatever peace of mind and carve-out of time they can yoke for themselves, so they may reinvigorate themselves and further contribute to the market of human capital when reenergized. Yes, even the evil humans who have sinned badly. But the collective human race? Well, we better collectively get off our asses pronto and elongate this ticking clock comprising mere centuries back into millennia.

And much to your enjoyment I'm sure, since I keep harping on concern for the end of all human existence, this is a nice place to roll into a discussion about death.

"It sure is!"

I have you frightened as all hell, and you are agreeing with me completely out of fear now, aren't you?

"Nooooo! [secretly nodding in the affirmative]"

Now I am become Death, the destroyer of worlds.

Often credited as the father of the atomic bomb for overseeing the Manhattan Project, J. Robert Oppenheimer uttered those exact words after the first A-bomb detonated in a New Mexico desert on July 16, 1945. He was quoting the Hindu text *Mahabharata*, and specifically a seven-hundred-verse scripture inside the text known as the *Bhagavad Gita*.

"And you're promulgating his quotation because you're about to make a larger point about death and nuclear power?"

Actually, no, we're clear that nuclear fusion is our next logical step toward Kardashev level advancement. I just thought it was a badass thing to utter at the time and wanted to share that he said it in case you didn't know.

"Oh."

What I really want to talk about is alkaline hydrolysis.

"That was my second guess."

Figured it was, Madame Curie.

Alkaline hydrolysis is also known as biocremation, resomation, flameless cremation, water cremation, and, finally, green cremation for its lesser carbon dioxide impact than other modes of human disposal. It reduces a body to components of liquid and bone, which is what naturally happens to a decomposing body anyway. Except, instead of taking roughly twenty-five years, it speeds up the process to between four and six hours. The remaining bone fragments can be dried and turned into a substance similar to cremated ashes if you'd like to have them.

"I think I know why you're telling me all this."

Enlighten me.

"It's a third side of the death argument, and it's becoming quite clear you like a good third side of any argument, lest we become too accustomed to only two black-and-white options. Democrats and Republicans come to mind."

Still listening.

"Burial and cremation are the two major options available on the market today, and this third option not only is better but also does not exist in a gray area, which your history of bullshitting has taught you is always the wrong option. And even though most people can't see it now, alkaline hydrolysis does not exist in a gray area, is truly better than the black-and-white options currently available, and should become the dominant path for human disposal for the betterment of all humankind."

You've rendered me speechless. And here I thought I had lost you.

"[Taking a bow]"

Well deserved! But there's more.

"Always is with you."

It's not simply that alkaline hydrolysis is better for the environment. It's that it's the perfect starting block for the change in mind-set humans need to make right now. It's the perfect starting block because it directly correlates with our final destination (death) and our most coveted way to remember our loved ones (death), and it forces us to face the inevitable for all of us (death). Yes, taxes, but still death. And perhaps most important, we are in desperate need of collective efficiency, a mode that will supercharge our focus on overall efficiency, as collective efficiency is our only option now.

3D printing. The Hyperloop. Blockchain. Self-driving cars. Flying taxis. Advanced solar and wind farms. Maybe even Dyson spheres someday…

"Except?"

Except what?

"Except you're about to tell me that although these are all awesome examples of efficiency, they will be wasted if we don't give them support."

Damn you are *en fuego*!

We are only ever as strong as our weakest link. Weak links like, say, the DMV hole-punching your license only to give you large pieces of environmentally unfriendly paper to carry around as an interim license while you await your new license hopefully arriving via archaic letter carrier a month later! Full-on fucking domiciles are being 3D-printed now, and Californian driver's licenses are getting hole-punched while we wait for new ones. Please, oh please, redirect all the monies from all our national treasury unto education and infrastructure. I beg of you. We mustn't dawdle. All available capital needs to secure our societal bottom so that the bottom can fall no lower. EVERYTHING we do from here on out should be as efficient as possible. The unmovable bureaucratic monoliths of our world must immediately disappear, and we must all prepare for the sexual robot revolution!

"Yes! Finally, the sex robots!"

Stick with me now, we're taking a real deep dive.

Bionics is *the science of constructing artificial systems that have some of the characteristics of living systems.* Engineered bionic replacement parts for humans now get a lot of love, and rightfully so. Dismembered war veterans, victims of horrific accidents that result in loss of vital human parts, or those born physically misconfigured are being fitted for bionic limbs, eyes, and spines daily. But what if someone simply WANTS to enhance themselves through bionics even though all their vital organs or limbs function perfectly? Naturally, the moral debates begin all over again. The stigmas are doled out like so many candies on Halloween. There is often very little love initially for groundbreaking scientific advances when they first appear. In vitro fertilization, stem cell research, cloning, release of synthetic life-forms into the wild, and gene splicing come to mind. Here we go again, with little initial love for the transhumanists of the world who recognize enhancing their bodies through technology could be our inevitable future.

"Hearing you loud and clear. Also, maybe a little more on that transhumanist word?"

Transhumanism is *the belief that the human race can evolve beyond its current physical and mental limitations, especially by means of science and technology*. Raymond Kurzweil is a transhumanist. Perhaps the most important person in the transhumanist movement. Kurzweil's first book, *The Age of Intelligent Machines,* was published in 1990 and starts with the assumption that a sufficiently advanced computer program could exhibit human-level intelligence. In 1999, he wrote *The Age of Spiritual Machines,* in which he presents his Law of Accelerating Returns to explain why important events happen more frequently as time moves on and why the computational capacity of computers increases exponentially.

"Science wins again, huh?"

One way or another, science always wins. Sometimes even science fiction.

In 1983, American science fiction author Vernor Vinge introduced the term *technological singularity* in the January issue of *Omni* magazine. He wrote: "We will soon create intelligences greater than our own. When this happens, human history will have reached a kind of singularity, an intellectual transition as impenetrable as the knotted space-time at the center of a black hole, and the world will pass far beyond our understanding." To be fair, it was in 1958 that Hungarian physicist and polymath John von Neumann was quoted as saying "the ever accelerating progress of technology…gives the appearance of approaching some essential singularity in history of the race beyond which human affairs, as we know them, could not continue." And though both of these men shall be given their respective due, it has been Raymond Kurzweil who has truly mainstreamed the ever-important concept. In 2006, he published *The Singularity Is Near: When Humans Transcend Biology.*

The singularity is now more than an abstraction; it is a predicted event when an artificial superintelligence will be introduced, prompting runaway technological growth that results in inconceivable changes to human civilization. Kurzweil predicts this event will happen in the year 2045. He's got a pretty fucking good track record of technological predictions so far.

"*Double gulp.*"

Now if I may, a great deal has recently been made of artificial intelligence (we're about to make a great deal of it ourselves), but I feel compelled to say this first: most of it leads us back to fear mongering. More specifically, the fear that machines (robots) will crush humans like the comparative ants we'll be once these robots acquire enough intelligence. It's possible that may very well happen, but we still need to press on anyway because we no longer have a choice. And we should further press on with unmitigated vigor in preparation for the time when humans will fuse with robotics and biologically transcend ourselves to endure.

"We really are there once again, aren't we?"

Where's that?

"Robert Johnson's crossroads."

Well, maybe not Johnson's exact crossroads, but yes, my friends, we are officially there.

Google CEO Sundar Pichai has already given us a pronounced credo as of January 2018, and for anyone who missed what he said—artificial intelligence is even more profound than fire. AI can eclipse what fire did for early humans, and contemporary humans have a chance to cultivate AI so that we may thrive, possibly even existing long enough to become the centerpiece species of a Type III civilization. As it stands now, the current AI in use is best likened to a fire cave dwellers might have made: social media feeds, music streaming, GPS navigation, facial recognition, Alexa, Cortana, Siri, and the like.

These are adorable little cave fires we can sleep comfortably around at night. They are twelve seconds of flight at Kitty Hawk. And yet, the roaring inferno at the belly of a steam engine is just around the bend, and we can't afford to miss that train when it comes to pick us up. We can't afford to shun AI's advancements because we are frightened by its effect on us. That fucking train is coming, and we need something that is going to make us all feel very comfortable about getting on board. Something way bigger than smartphones and smart cars. Something even the staunchest of Luddites might get excited about.

"I can't believe I'm about to say this…"

Say it. It will feel so liberating.

"We need a freaking android sexual revolution!"

Hallelujah! That wasn't so bad, was it?

"Surprisingly not so bad."

Seriously, this is not something I take lightly or am totally amusing myself writing about. It was hard enough to chronicle the demise of football's national dominance, let alone predict that the rise of human-to-robot relations will be our next version of the space race. But I'm predicting it anyway, and I take you back to bionics as the crux of said prediction.

"Engineered replacement parts for victims is all good, but what if someone WANTS to enhance themselves, right? The stigmas are doled out like so many candies on Halloween."

Exactly. There is often very little love for groundbreaking scientific augmentation when it first appears, but eventually beneficial augmentations become the norm. Robot love will too. As will more people "hacking" their own bodies for heightened sexual gratification. Yet, those are just the precursors to the ultimate norm. The ultimate norm is going to be some combination of organic and inorganic life—especially when the singularity arrives, lest we be swept away with the tide by letting AI take over everything entirely. Artificial intelligence is here, the singularity WILL happen, but it is up to us to remain a step ahead of the androids. The good news is that this is absolutely possible and our most likely outcome.

"How?"

Because no matter how many lifelike algorithms we implant in them, they will never be us. They will never achieve full consciousness. Yes, humans will eventually fuse ourselves with inorganic parts to keep up, and yes, we will eventually create more ways to elongate life, but just as assuredly robots will always be just that…robots.

"I'm not sure I'm ready to take that risk."

You don't have a choice; the race is already afoot! Baidu, Alibaba, and Tencent aren't just platforms for consumerism, they are havens for advancements in artificial intelligence, and they are also properties of one very rigid empire that doesn't seem all that interested in ever playing second fiddle to any other empire. An empire that is about to roll out a dystopian Social Ranking System in Beijing (as a test city) with the help of artificial intelligence by 2021. Emmanuel Macron has pledged $1.5 billion from public coffers to boost France's contribution to advancing artificial intelligence. Japan now has a humanoid robot that installs drywall autonomously. And, of course, our very own Silicon Valley is rife with startups focused solely on gargantuan leaps in AI. Not just Silicon Valley, mind you—MIT's Boston Dynamics currently leads the charge with its androids SpotMini and Atlas making towering autonomous leaps by the month now.

"This is really happening. I can't believe this is really happening..."

Welcome it in. You are prepared to emerge victorious in your imminent future. I know you are. Come on now, let's hear it. Let's hear what victory sounds like.

"Recognize that living is suffering but can be made meaningful if I stand for something."

Yes.

"Forgo false deities yet remain steadfast to a humanistic code of conduct."

Starting to feel it...

"Respect my own vulnerabilities and take time for self-reflection whenever possible."

You just keep on preaching now...

"Admit my shortcomings and seek parity among all races, genders, and ethnicities."

[Uncontrollably swaying to the brilliance of your gospel]

"Collaborate with every generation from all walks of life to ensure our survival together."

This could be the best sermon I've ever been to.

"Commit only to capitalism and apply the riches to education and technology above all."

I might be losing consciousness soon!

"Welcome sexualized robots into my home in the next couple of years."

Ummmmmm, let's try that last one again.

"Reconstruct my own middle-class morality to meet the future head-on, understand that in the face of catastrophic climate change human avarice is an imperative from here on out, someday welcome transhumanism as a necessary counter to artificial intelligence's coming technological upheaval, and hold fast the notion that the continued thriving of *Homo sapiens* is what matters most."

Praise! Praise! Praise! Praise! Praise! Praise! Praise! Amen.

Who's the protagonist?

"I am."

Couldn't hear you there. I said, WHO'S THE PROTAGONIST?

"I AM!"

Fucking-A right you are. We will never acquiesce to any tide, let alone an impending automaton tsunami, because we are the protagonists, never anyone else. The amount of cosmic time it took to get here and have our moment on this ball of silicon, iron, magnesium, and aluminum cannot be for naught. All of that prodigious nitrogen formulating inside life-giving amino acids it took so we can stand here now and shout these words from a mountaintop cannot simply fade away. Our instant to bask in the awe-inspiring and nurturing glow of that exquisite churning globule, the one that looks especially prepossessing while sipping a morning java as it rises over the sea, is not over. Not without one hell of a fight!

"And so—we finally get to battle."

You, me, Churchill, Captain Kirk, Sulu, Chekov, Uhura, McCoy, Scotty, Nurse Chapel, everyone. Even Spock. It's a battle for our souls, and it sure as hell isn't with each other, or androids—it is a conflict deep within. It takes an elephantine shift in mind-set to want to unmask inner truth. It takes the self-detonation of a sizable quake to reveal raw certitudes. It takes releasing truth, and only truth, to emerge soul intact in the face of our own incongruity. Victory, as it were, takes a fierce personal grappling with paradox.

"Hand me that rope, hang me by a tree, and leave me be for a little while."

Here, take my rope and tree. You've earned them.

"Thrive we aspire. Thrive we must."

Believe it.

CHAPTER NINE

AN OPTIMISTIC PRAGMATIST

DURING MY WIFE'S pregnancy, I accompanied her on many an ob-gyn visit. The construct of the office was such that we'd start on one floor where the blood testing and ultrasounds took place for all patients of the very large practice, and then we'd head to another floor to see her doctor in a much more personal office. That office had its own bathroom for patients, and it was in this bathroom that I discovered a surprising impetus for this book. An impetus that hangs right above the toilet, as a matter of fact. A toilet painting of all things.

It reads: "Anyone can slay a dragon, he told me, but try waking up every morning and loving the world all over again. That's what takes a real hero."

Brian Andreas (pen name of American author Kai Andreas Skye) said that.

I'm not going to pretend like this quote found on this particular toilet painting is some incredible secret tucked away in the bathroom of a doctor's office. No, you can apparently find the quote on all types of commercialized crap, such as keychains, mugs, and even lunchbox covers. But that's not where I found it.

I found it above an ob-gyn's toilet, right where I needed to find it, during one of the happiest times of my life. Voilà, a book is born.

Anyone can slay a dragon, he told me.

Odin captured my respect for mythological figures, and so too do dragons. Horned, winged beasts breathing fire. Depictions of our greatest distractions. Destroyers of the highest order. Encapsulation, in a way, of all that befalls us, constantly roaring to be slain.

The din of a dragon is overbearing. Always, before the fire, comes the din. The dragon circles its prey, screeching malevolently, frightening and confusing its victims, cajoling them to abandon the safety of their hiding spaces. And when there's more than one dragon, the din is mind-throbbingly painful. A cacophony of agonizing sounds. Climate, politics, economics, media, race, religion, terrorism, nationalism, tribalism, technology. They circle in formation, squawking for us to come out and bow before them. Bow, cower, quiver, beg, plead, and supplicate for our lives. But the dragons don't listen. They only incinerate. So, we reassemble, and we arm ourselves, and we pair off, conspiring in our little groups how best to defeat them. Except, now we're divided, making it that much easier for the dragons to defeat us. And that's the real problem, isn't it? Anyone can slay a dragon, so maybe we should stop dividing ourselves trying to slay them in the first place. Now we know better. We know simply to honor them instead.

Respect, admire, recognize the burdensome beasts. We know it's not easy to do that when they are shrieking and we are scared. But we don't run out to them. We don't fall prey to their tricks to get us out into the open. We stand firm, suspend ourselves upside down, and see them for what they really are—paragons of chaos that must feast on our flesh to remain alive. We listen to them bellow from our new vantage point, and we no longer hear beckoning malevolence—we hear the fearful whimper of a hungry animal. We remain dangled long enough, doing nothing but listening, *not even listening but being quiet, still, and solitary*, and we will not be disfigured by the battle with a dragon—we will instead remain unblemished, rewarded with truths about their elemental lack of power over us in the first place. Best of all, we know now that the battle was never with these dragons; it is always with ourselves.

I wrote this book to promote a dissident perspective on life, yes. To stir up a bubbling cauldron of critical thought, throwing in ingredient after ingredient, absolutely. But I also wrote this book to do my part in helping prepare for the extraordinary changes the world is about to encounter. Crescendoing to a notion of technological upheaval such as the singularity without first layering in a means to meet it head-on would have been irresponsible. We absolutely need to toughen ourselves mentally, financially, and spiritually, even if we can't predict a firm timeline or what the world will really look like after its arrival. And, sure, some readers will choose not to believe a word of this. They will liken this to doomsday predictions that never happen (2012, True Way, Millerism, Y2K). That's cool, except clearly none of the aforementioned is about doomsday at all, and artificial intelligence is incontestably here already. I'm just one in a long line of earthly citizens who want the best for humanity, and I wanted to help filter the forest through the trees so we can incontrovertibly wrap our heads around the explosion of change on the horizon.

And, no, I'm clearly not Hawking, Dawkins, Doudna, Bonner, Venter, Witten, Guinn, Oxman, Degrasse Tyson, Harris, Chambon, or Seager. I am in fact a broker of private wealth and a proud bartender. But this time? This actually made me the best person for the job. This one didn't need to come from a guru, celebrity, former government official, ex-military, or a PhD. This one needed to come from an individual who bleeds contradiction. Someone who's worked at both the world's premiere entertainment agency and world's largest entertainment studio, yet who has also waited hand and foot on neo-Nazis. Someone who has skied the back of a Canadian glacier but also tasted the wretched bile of crippling financial debt. Someone who's rafted class-five rapids on a Colombian river but also stolen laundry quarters from a good friend to buy one-dollar chicken sandwiches at Jack-In-The-Box to avoid starvation. Someone who's hang-glided off a Swiss mountain but also pick-axed a fresh grave for the dog of a porn director in hundred-degree heat while wearing a business suit when a realty listing appointment got REAL strange. Three-Michelin-star feasts in Japan, exquisite vacations across the Orient, the rarified air inside Teatro Colon—shady midnight notarizations, autoimmune disease rabbit holes with uncertified practitioners, Vegas at 4:11 a.m. on a Wednesday. That's right, someone who's really lived both sides of the coin. Wagered with the French Riviera's elite but also wasted days in low-end poker dens. Pled for salvation at Jerusalem's Wailing Wall only to later find solace in secularism. No, the good people didn't need to hear from another member of just the bourgeoisie on this one. This time a weathered voice of the proletariat needed a say. This one had to come from the heart.

Now gather the fuck back around if you will, because we're not quite done here.

Chances are, after (or maybe by the time) you read this, we will be in a worldwide recession. No one knows how light or harsh it will be, but that's not what's most important. What's most important is that, as we slog through this one, we finally have the right debates about what best to do with our global resources for the brightest possible future.

Undoubtedly, the calls for universal basic income are going to get louder as the economic pain intensifies. That's all well and good, but UBI is wasted money if big enough advancements in artificial intelligence don't bring the cost of living way down. Like, way, way, way the fuck down. So far down that basic necessities no longer cost the middle class 70 percent of their monthly nut but more like 7 percent (total arbitrary number, but the symmetry of the sentence should prove my point). UBI is socialist delusion without the money meant for it being put to highest and best use. This means that the next advancements in AI must not only take over half of jobs in the next quarter century but also bring down the cost of everything too. There are already growing shortages of farmers, house appraisers, airline pilots, and doctors and nurses, to name a few. Hell, even ecologically valuable insect species are dwindling rapidly. The AI that replaces them (among legions of other positions on a grand scale) must bring the costs that those positions incurred down too.

This means that the rich (and super-rich) who will control the artificial intelligence are just going to continue to get richer. Yep, an even bigger gap in the top few percent is coming. Guess what? I don't care, and nor should you. As long as they must function under the laws of a democratic society and not rule us like monarchs, they are more than welcome to have gazillions of dollars and drink Armand de Brignac off each other aboard eighty-thousand-foot yachts. We're all wasting time getting bent about the ever-widening gap, but what was the number that was ever okay to begin with? Five times as rich? Ten times? A million times? Capitalism is inevitably going to create a One Percent, regardless of how much of the available money that One Percent controls or doesn't control. Let them have their twelve mansions…the rest of us need basic necessities at costs we can afford so we may maintain a middle class.

Because, though it will be hard to believe this now, if we are successful in altering what it means to be middle class by way of artificial intelligence taking over half the world's workforce, subsequently gashing our cost of living and possibly paving the way for an entitlement (UBI) that would make some sense for once, this would be enormously freeing. Our time and energy spent on commonplace activities can be applied elsewhere, and we can actually pursue dreams that so many who are currently economically and racially suppressed have never had the chance to do.

Moreover, remember this while you're weighing the tempered yet realistic version of Shangri-La I'm selling here: advancements in technology have historically been way more beneficial to expanding our societies, bringing us all closer to being even a Type 0.7 civilization, than they have been at pushing us aside entirely. The Renaissance, the Industrial Revolution, the space race, and, oh, let's say, online banking come to mind. Artificial intelligence can do the same if we apply our resources appropriately. AI has the potential to equalize life basics while still having us all feel useful in a capitalist civilization. That's fucking huge, good people. Huge because once our tolerance for technology expands and our productivity increases, our chance of survival heightens. Survival…

Willfully letting the robots take over is only half the story. The other half is utilizing them correctly to endure (even possibly alter back in our favor) the coming climate catastrophe if we stay here or utilizing them correctly to jettison ourselves toward the stars to avoid the climate catastrophe altogether. A bump of one degree Celsius to the earth's average temperature has already been confirmed, and yep, we were the ones who bumped it. Another degree bump and life for all starts to get REALLY unpleasant. Another degree bump after that and mass human migrations start taking place. Two more degree bumps after that? Good night to most organic matter.

Much like the singularity, that second degree bump is right around the cosmic corner. And considering I posited a belief that our collective sixth senses have been sounding alarm bells for centuries already, you think perhaps I also believe the singularity and impending climate cataclysm have more to do with each other than just an insanely fortuitous enmeshment of cosmic timing? Dharma, my friends. Cosmic law and order. You've heard me say money is the great equalizer twice before, so here's me saying it a third time. And I say it because money is math, and math is the only language that everyone on the planet can speak concurrently. Math is the one true universal language, money is its mouthpiece, and all the money in the world should be redirected at artificial intelligence and all educational curriculums that support AI vocation. It's our last best chance.

Human beings are playing with "house money" now. Evolving as we did, first from eukaryotes and later apes, only to go on a nearly twenty-million-year run of outlasting every other genus at the blackjack table—I'd say we earned quite a big pile of house money. But house money can be dangerous. It even has a malady named after it: *the House Money Effect*. Essentially, you pocket the original money you started with, and then you get aggressive with the money you were up. That aggression leads to losing the house money, and the sour taste of that loss leads to digging back in your pocket for your original stack. Naturally, you should have walked away when you were up in the first place, and now you are most likely going to lose your original stack after you bring it back out. Sit at the table long enough, and the house wins. The house always wins—hence that charming fucking term.

Humans have a very difficult time walking away. We are, by nature, irrational optimists. Another not so nice way of saying it is that we are delusional. That lovable delusion of ours is why casinos were invented in the first place. Palaces of sport, leisure, gaming, chance (what our inner algorithms yearn for), but most of all, palaces of grand delusion. It's also why we find ourselves in the heap of climatological trouble we are in now. Well, the time of delusion is over. Billion-dollar Powerball lotteries aren't going to do a damn thing to change lives, nor are we going to change the course of our future for the better by ourselves. We need to hang ourselves upside down once more and shuck irrational optimism. We need optimistic pragmatism in its stead. We need logicality. We need to get avaricious. We need our new "fire." We need AI.

Try waking up every morning and loving the world all over again.

I am indeed a cynical Xer, but you know me well by now, so you know I harbor no cynicism for these motivational words. I harbor no cynicism for love. On the contrary, I burn an *intense feeling of deep affection* for the truths uncovered in our contradictions—the definition of love. I've ardently entreated clichéd quotes from some of the more go-to historical figures (Socrates, Churchill, Kafka), and I ardently propagate the same with love. *Love is an open door, love means never having to say you're sorry, and love conquers all.* Love is why when I look at the summary of our plight as humans, I see an unquenchable desire for the common good. We may otherwise appear divided and brutal as all hell, but the underlying empathy that nurtures the common good is why Hanged Man always emerges victorious, why humans have made it even this far in history, and why we stand a great chance of continuing for eons to come.

"It was the Buddha who said *true love is born from understanding.*"

Oh, hey, welcome back! And quoting the Buddha no less.

"Apparently, he was pretty wise."

I'm really going to miss you.

"Back at ya, Pfeffer. But I do have one last question."

Anything. Shoot.

"The book's title?"

Ah, yes, the title. And an excellent segue to the final part of Brian Andreas's quote.

That's what takes a real hero.

In 1384, English priest and influential dissident John Wycliffe translated the Bible, and in his prologue, he noted: "The Bible is for the Government of the people, by the people, and for the people." Nearly five hundred years later, a thoughtful and powerful leader emerged and invoked Wycliffe's message at a time of immense strife in our country. The Great Emancipator Abraham Lincoln was an advocate of truth and justice. A torchbearer of human parity. A certifiable hero of critical thought. And he ever so eloquently enshrined these words as a zealous pledge to democracy when he delivered his famous Gettysburg Address:

"...shall have a new birth of freedom, and that government of the people, by the people, and for the people shall not perish from the earth."

Shall not perish from the earth.

SHALL NOT PERISH...from the earth.

Be good to each other out there, Hanged People. Be good to yourselves.

And above all else, thrive.

Above all else...

Prosper Today. Perpetuate Tomorrow.

Onward.

THE END

ACKNOWLEDGMENTS

Let's start with Naomi Eagleson and her company, The Artful Editor. When figuring out how to get this damn thing published, I stumbled upon her website and reached out with many a question. Lucky for me, she had many an answer, and all of them delivered with patience and professionalism, which meant a great deal to this book-world neophyte. Once hired, Naomi then paired me with editor extraordinaire Christina Palaia. Christina took a heart-filled first draft and expertly crafted it into a focused manuscript. We're talking knife-like precision. So, thank you, both Naomi and Christina, for your tremendous guidance, deft counsel, and hard work.

To J. Maarten Troost. Nope, never met the man, but *The Sex Lives of Cannibals* was the book I read just before writing this one, and he showed me that a little humor and a fair amount of focused stream of consciousness can go a long way. To Yuval Noah Harari. Never met him either, and probably never will, but I wasn't bullshitting when I said *Sapiens* and *Homo Deus* had a major impact on my life. Even better, after the first draft of this book was completed (around June 2018), and as I waited for edits to come back from Christina, I read *21 Lessons for the 21st Century*. Yeah, it's a fucking amazing book, and more than anything, it gave me great confidence that the bulk of what I had already written was on the right track. I can only dream that the perspective expressed in this book helps further and enhance what Harari consistently promulgates.

To an anonymous psychic woman who just happened to be at a popup store on Melrose Avenue in January 2018 when my wife and I were taking our son for a walk. Perhaps I'll one day share an incredible yarn of cosmic serendipity around this with those who care to listen. Even more than Brian Andreas, this person ignited the writing of this book, so, thank you very much, Random Psychic on Melrose (of all places!). Maybe I'll have a chance to thank you in person someday.

To my business partner, Andrew. Since 2006, we have been through some serious shit together. Ideas, debt, businesses, climbing out of said debt, starting our own respective families. John D. Rockefeller once noted: *A friendship founded on business is better than a business founded on friendship.* Well, what started out as like-minded business ideals has flourished into a great friendship. And while he's a hell of a partner, he's an even better friend. To all my friends, and specifically my three closest friends, Jeremy, Paul, and Adam, who have each contributed a great deal to my personal growth. Friends naturally wish the best for you, good friends legitimately care about your well-being, but best friends challenge you to be the best version of yourself. These three bring the funk.

To those mentioned peripherally and sporadically throughout the book. Known figures got some specific shout-outs by name, but plenty more, including plenty of people close to me whose names I didn't include in case you wouldn't have wanted your name in print…thank you.

To my test readers. Your quick reads and outstanding notes were much appreciated. Thank you very much for your time, attention, and excellent thoughts.

To my in-laws, Kathy and Brian. Nope, not a misprint. Love my in-laws! Supportive doesn't begin to describe the depths of their contributions, and I thank them from the bottom of my heart for understanding why I needed to write and then publish this thing. To my own parents, Ilene and Barry. I mean, they only raised me and funded countless edifying life endeavors and showered me with love for forty years and been nothing but encouraging voices of parental guidance. Nothing major. Ha. Thank you, *padres.*

To my brother, Dan, who whether he knows it or not has been the inspiration for EVERYTHING I have ever done in my life. Everyone needs a wartime consigliere. He is mine. Brothers-in-arms for eternity. To his wife, Heather, who is also my de facto sister now. Not sister-in-law. Sister. A cancer-fighting warrior. Show me a greater lover of humanity. I dare you. To my nieces and nephew, Xylie, Samantha, and Harley. Before my own son came along, they were my children too. Still are. Always will be.

And, finally, to my splendiferous wife, Shannon, and our great joy, Ellis. I could spend ten more pages gushing about you both, but I hope it's better to sum up how I feel in a simple statement of truth that powers me through every great day: I cease to exist without you. You are now the heart of who I am. I love you both beyond. Thank you.

REFERENCES AND RESOURCES

INTRODUCTION

Trainspotting and Year 1996

Trainspotting. Dir. Danny Boyle. Polygram Filmed Entertainment and Miramax Films. 1996

DDC Public Affairs. "20 Things That Happened in 1996." *https://ddcpublicaffairs.com/20-things-in-1996/*

People History. "What Happened in 1996?" *http://www.thepeoplehistory.com/1996.html*

On This Day. "Historical Events in 1996." *https://www.onthisday.com/events/date/1996*

Infoplease. "Top News Stories from 1996." *https://www.infoplease.com/year/1996*

Wikipedia. "1996 in the United States." *https://en.wikipedia.org/wiki/1996*

The Hanged Man and Odin

Bunning, Joan. "The Hanged Man." *http://www.learntarot.com/maj12.htm*

Rioux, James. "The Hanged Man." *http://www.ata-tarot.com/resource/cards/maj12.html*

Labrynthios. "The Hanged Man Meaning—Major Arcana Tarot Card Meanings." *https://labyrinthos.co/blogs/tarot-card-meanings-list/the-hanged-man-meaning-major-arcana-tarot-card-meanings*

Numerologysign. "The Hanged Man Tarot Card Meaning Upright and Reversed." *https://numerologysign.com/tarot/card-meanings/major-arcana/hanged-man/*

Norse Mythology. "Odin's Discovery of the Runes." *https://norse-mythology.org/tales/odins-discovery-of-the-runes/*

Evolve+Ascend. "Odin and The Hanged Man: Time to Face the Fear." *http://www.evolveandascend.com/2016/04/05/odin-hanged-man-time-face-fear/*

Ancient Pages. "God of the Gallows and How Odin Hanged Himself from Yggdrasil to Know Secrets of Runes." *http://www.ancientpages.com/2018/05/07/god-of-the-gallows-and-how-odin-hanged-himself-from-yggdrasil-to-know-secrets-of-runes/*

CHAPTER 1

Buddhism, Dharma, the Four Noble Truths, Siddhartha, Man's Search for Meaning

Buddhist Center. "Buddhism for Today." *https://thebuddhistcentre.com/buddhism*

About Buddhism. "About Buddhism." *http://www.aboutbuddhism.org/*

Diamond Way Buddhism. "What Is Buddhism?" *https://www.diamondway-buddhism.org/buddhism/*

Pew Research Center. "Buddhists." December 18, 2012. *http://www.pewforum.org/2012/12/18/global-religious-landscape-exec/*

Reach to Teach. "Religion in Thailand." *https://www.reachtoteachrecruiting.com/guides/thailand/religion-in-thailand/*

Ray, Reginald. "What Is Dharma?" Lion's Roar. December 26, 2017. *https://www.lionsroar.com/in-a-word-dharma/*

Buswell, Robert E., and Donald S. Lopez Jr. "The Many Meanings of Dharma." *Tricycle*, Spring, 2014. *https://tricycle.org/magazine/many-meanings-dharma/*

McLeod, Melvin. "What Are the Four Noble Truths?" Lion's Roar. March 12, 2018. *https://www.lionsroar.com/what-are-the-four-noble-truths/*

Hesse, Hermann. *Siddhartha*. New Directions Publishing, 1992.

Frankl, Viktor E. *Man's Search for Meaning*. Beacon Press, 1959.

Burton, Neel. "Man's Search for Meaning: Meaning as a Cure for Depression and Other Ills." Psychology Today. Updated September 17, 2017. *https://www.psychologytoday.com/us/blog/hide-and-seek/201205/mans-search-meaning*

Entrepreneurship, Hustling, September 2008, Reactive Arthritis, Subprime Lending, Fantastic Four, Part 2: Rise of the Silver Surfer, My Super Ex-Girlfriend

English Oxford Living Dictionaries. "Entrepreneur." *https://en.oxforddictionaries.com/definition/us/entrepreneur*

English Oxford Living Dictionaries. "Hustler." *https://en.oxforddictionaries.com/definition/us/hustler*

Dictionary.com. "Hustler." *https://www.dictionary.com/browse/hustler*

Amadeo, Kimberly. "2008 Financial Crisis Timeline: 37 Critical Events in the Worst Crisis Since the Depression." The Balance. Updated October 13, 2018. *https://www.thebalance.com/2008-financial-crisis-timeline-3305540*

On This Day. "Historical Events in September 2008." *https://www.onthisday.com/events/date/2008/september*

National Organization for Rare Disorders. "Reactive Arthritis." *https://rarediseases.org/rare-diseases/reactive-arthritis/*

Cedars-Sinai. "Reactive Arthritis (Reiter's Syndrome)." *https://www.cedars-sinai.org/health-library/diseases-and-conditions/r/reactive-arthritis-reiters-syndrome.html*

Campbell, Dakin, and Jennifer Surane. "Subprime Lending." Bloomberg News. Updated January 2, 2018. *https://www.bloomberg.com/quicktake/subprime-lending*

Fantastic 4: Rise of the Silver Surfer. Dir. Tim Story. 20th Century Fox, 2007.

My Super Ex-Girlfriend. Dir. Ivan Reitman. 20th Century Fox, 2006.

Ratings Agencies, 2008 Retirement Investments, CDOs, The Big Short, 2007 Mortgage Crisis, Brokers, Real Estate Investing: BRRRR, CA Salespersons, and Broker License

Reuters. "Moody's $864M Penalty for Rating's Runup to 2008 Financial Crisis." *The Guardian* (Manchester). January 14, 2017. *https://www.theguardian.com/business/2017/jan/14/moodys-864m-penalty-for-ratings-in-run-up-to-2008-financial-crisis*

Singletary, Michelle. "10 Years After the Financial Crisis, Has Your Retirement Portfolio Recovered?" *Washington Post.* September 10, 2018. *https://www.washingtonpost.com/business/2018/09/10/years-after-financial-crisis-has-your-retirement-portfolio-recovered/?utm_term=.1e1ffa677516*

Gagliano, Rico. "Financial Crisis 101: CDOs Explained." Marketplace. October 3, 2008. *https://www.market-*

place.org/2008/10/03/business/fallout-financial-crisis/financial-crisis-101-cdos-explained

Lewis, Michael. *The Big Short.* W. W. Norton and Company, March 2010.

The Big Short. Dir. Adam McKay. Paramount Pictures, December 2015.

Pritchard, Justin. "The Mortgage Crisis Explained: What Caused the Mortgage Crisis?" The Balance. Updated May 11, 2018. *https://www.thebalance.com/mortgage-crisis-overview-315684*

Hall, Mary. "Who Is to Blame for the Subprime Crisis?" Investopedia. Updated March 23, 2018. *https://www.investopedia.com/articles/07/subprime-blame.asp*

Lander, Steve. "What Is a Wholesale Mortgage Loan?" The Nest. *https://budgeting.thenest.com/wholesale-mortgage-loan-32255.html*

California Department of Real Estate. "Requirements to Apply for a Real Estate Salespersons License." *http://www.bre.ca.gov/Examinees/RequirementsSales.html*

California Department of Real Estate. "Requirements to Apply for a Real Estate Broker License." *http://www.dre.ca.gov/examinees/requirementsbroker.html*

Syrios, Andrew. "The BRRRR (Buy, Rehab, Rent, Refinance, Repeat) Strategy: A Primer for Investors." Bigger Pockets. *https://www.biggerpockets.com/renewsblog/brrrr-buyrehabrentrefinancerepeatprimer/*

The Sunset Marquis Hotel, Jerry Leiber, The Flamingo Kid, Only by the Night, Matthew McConaughey, CA First-Degree Murder, Law & Order

Baum, Gary, and Gary Walker. "Sunset Marquis: Secrets of Rock 'n' Roll's Wild Ride." *Hollywood Reporter.* February 8, 2013. *https://www.hollywoodreporter.com/news/sunset-marquis-secrets-rock-n-419290*

Ankeny, Jason. "The Secret Behind This Legendary Hollywood Hotel's 50-Year Run." *Entrepreneur Magazine*. February 1, 2014. *https://www.entrepreneur.com/article/229722*

Sunset Marquis: History. "If These Walls Could Rock." *https://sunsetmarquis.com/about-west-hollywood-hotel/history/*

Wikipedia. "Sunset Marquis Hotel." *https://en.wikipedia.org/wiki/Sunset_Marquis_Hotel*

Upscale Living Magazine. "Sunset Marquis Unveils Stunning Property Remodel." *https://www.upscalelivingmag.com/sunset-marquis-unveils-stunning-property-remodel/*

Leiber & Stoller. Homepage. *http://w.leiberstoller.com/Home.html*

The Flamingo Kid. Dir. Garry Marshall. 20th Century Fox, 1984.

Only by the Night. Kings of Leon. Blackbird Studios. The Control Group, RCA, September 2008.

IMDb. "Matthew McConaughey." *https://www.imdb.com/name/nm0000190/*

Kurutz, Steven. "The Tao of Matthew McConaughey." *New York Times*. December 8, 2016. *https://www.nytimes.com/2016/12/08/fashion/mens-style/the-tao-of-matthew-mcconaughey.html*

FindLaw. "California First Degree Murder Laws." *https://statelaws.findlaw.com/california-law/california-first-degree-murder-laws.html*

LawTech Publishing Group. *2018 California Penal Code: Unabridged*. 2018.

Law & Order. Created by Dick Wolf. NBC Universal Television, 1988.

CHAPTER 2

Dragnet, Paganism, Emperor Constantine, Illegitimate, Religious Heads of State

Dragnet. Dir. Tom Mankiewicz. Universal Pictures, 1987.

All About Spirituality. "Paganism." *https://www.allaboutspirituality.org/paganism.htm*

BBC: Religions. "Paganism." 2014. *http://www.bbc.co.uk/religion/religions/paganism/*

Pagan Federation. "What Is Paganism?" *http://www.paganfederation.org/what-is-paganism/*

Von Mosheim, Johann Lorenz. "Conversion of Constantine: Decline of Paganism." History World International Project. *http://history-world.org/christianity%20conversion_of_constantine.htm*

WordAtlas. "What Is Paganism?" *https://www.worldatlas.com/articles/what-is-paganism.html*

Merriam-Webster. "Illegitimate." *https://www.merriam-webster.com/dictionary/illegitimate*

Theodorou, Angelina E. "In 30 Countries, Heads of States Must Belong to a Certain Religion." Pew Research Center. July 22, 2014. *http://www.pewresearch.org/fact-tank/2014/07/22/in-30-countries-heads-of-state-must-belong-to-a-certain-religion/*

Examples of Religions, Xenu, Scientific Kingdoms, Judaism, Brit Milah, Creationism

Crabtree, Vexen. "A List of All Religions and Belief Systems." Human Truth Foundation. 2013. *http://www.humanreligions.info/religions.html*

Sartore, Melissa. "Details You Never Knew About the Surprisingly Thorough History of Xenu, Scientology's

Galactic Ruler." Weird History. *https://www.ranker.com/list/facts-about-xenu-in-scientology/melissa-sartore*

Bailey, Regina. "The 6 Kingdoms of Life." ThoughtCo. Updated October 5, 2018. *https://www.thoughtco.com/six-kingdoms-of-life-373414*

History Channel. "Judaism." A&E Television Networks. Updated August 23, 2018. *https://www.history.com/topics/religion/judaism*

Chabad Org. "The Circumcision Ceremony." *https://www.chabad.org/library/article_cdo/aid/1472861/jewish/The-Circumcision-Ceremony.htm*

Encyclopaedia Britannica. "Creationism." *https://www.britannica.com/topic/creationism*

Human Capital, the Soul, Consciousness, Life Cycles, Time As an Abstract, Lord Tennyson

Huff, Richard. "Human Capital." Encyclopaedia Britannica. October 4, 2018. *https://www.britannica.com/topic/human-capital*

Lion's Roar Staff. "Do Buddhists Believe in a Soul?" August 2, 2017. *https://www.lionsroar.com/do-buddhists-believe-in-a-soul/*

Quora. "Where Is the Soul Located in the Body? In the Brain? In the Heart?" *https://www.quora.com/Where-is-the-soul-located-in-the-body-In-the-brain-In-the-heart*

Rothman, Joshua. "Daniel Dennett's Science of the Soul: A Philosopher's Lifelong Quest to Understand the Making of the Mind." *The New Yorker*. March 27, 2017. *https://www.newyorker.com/magazine/2017/03/27/daniel-dennetts-science-of-the-soul*

Parks, Jake. "All Disk Galaxies Rotate Once Every Billion Years." Astronomy. March 13, 2018. *http://www.astronomy.com/news/2018/03/all-galaxies-rotate-once-every-billion-years*

Frank, Adam. "There Is No Such Thing as Time." *Popular Science*. September 18, 2012. *https://www.popsci.com/science/article/2012-09/book-excerpt-there-no-such-thing-time*

BrainyQuote. "Norman Cousins Quotes." *https://www.brainyquote.com/quotes/norman_cousins_121747*

The New York Jets, CTE and Its Effects, Players with CTE, Decline in Football Participation, Fans Abandoning NFL, Concussion Settlements with NFL, Violence in Buddhism, Games

Barra, Allen. "Why the New York Jets Have Been Bad for So Long." *The Atlantic*. November 29, 2013. *https://www.theatlantic.com/entertainment/archive/2013/11/why-the-new-york-jets-have-been-so-bad-for-so-long/281917/*

Concussion Legacy Foundation. "What Is CTE?" *https://concussionfoundation.org/CTE-resources/what-is-CTE*

Moran, Barbara. "CTE Found in 99 Percent of Former NFL Players Studied." Boston University Research. July 24, 2017. *https://www.bu.edu/research/articles/cte-former-nfl-players/*

Duaine Hahn, Jason. "Jason Hairston Had CTE Symptoms Before Death—Here Are Other Football Players Who Had the Disease." *People Magazine*. September 7, 2017. *https://people.com/sports/prominent-nfl-players-diagnosed-with-cte-the-degenerative-brain-disease/*

Rettner, Rachael. "Aaron Hernandez Had 'Severe' Form of Brain Disease. What Is CTE?" Live Science. September 22, 2017.

https://www.livescience.com/60492-aaron-hernandez-brain-severe-cte.html

Keilman, John. "Youth Football Participation Declines as Worries Mount About Concussions, CTE." *Chicago Tribune.* September 5, 2017. *https://www.chicagotribune.com/news/local/breaking/ct-football-youth-decline-met-20170904-story.html*

Ozanian, Mike. "NFL Sale Prices Being Hurt by League's Declining Popularity." *Forbes.* June 2, 2018. *https://www.forbes.com/sites/mikeozanian/2018/06/02/nfl-sale-prices-being-hurt-by-leagues-declining-popularity/#21f342dd7e94*

Stites, Adam. "How the NFL Can Help Save Itself from Itself." SB Nation. August 29, 2018. *https://www.sbnation.com/2018/8/29/17405754/2018-nfl-preview-how-the-nfl-can-help-save-itself-politics-trump*

CBS News. "Claims in NFL Concussion Settlement Hit $500 Million in Less Than 2 Years." AP Wire. July 30, 2018. *https://www.cbsnews.com/news/nfl-concussion-claims-hit-500-million-less-than-2-years/*

Arnold, Dan, and Alicia Turner. "Why Are We Surprised When Buddhists Are Violent?" *New York Times,* Opinion Section. March 5, 2018. *https://www.nytimes.com/2018/03/05/opinion/buddhists-violence-tolerance.html*

Lents, Nathan H. "Why Play Is Important." Psychology Today. May 1, 2017. *https://www.psychologytoday.com/us/blog/beastly-behavior/201705/why-play-is-important*

Football Global Reach, NFL Broadcast and Television Content, NFL On-Field Injuries

Seifert, Kevin. "Planet Football: Top Countries Where the Sport Is Thriving." ABC News. November 26, 2016. *https://abc-*

news.go.com/Sports/planet-football-top-countries-sport-thriving/story?id=43791082

NFL.com. "Impact of Television." *https://operations.nfl.com/the-game/impact-of-television/*

Marks, Brendan. "Injuries Happen in Sports, Especially Football, but NFL This Year Can't Be Overlooked." *Charlotte Observer.* Updated October 18, 2017. *https://www.charlotteobserver.com/sports/nfl/carolina-panthers/article179229321.html*

CHAPTER 3

Social Viewpoints, Second Amendment, NRA, National Firearms Act, Gun Control Act 1968

Student News Daily. "Conservative vs. Liberal Beliefs." Updated 2010. *https://www.studentnewsdaily.com/conservative-vs-liberal-beliefs/*

FindLaw. "Second Amendment—U.S. Constitution: Second Amendment—Bearing Arms." *https://constitution.findlaw.com/amendment2.html*

National Rifle Association. "A Brief History of the NRA." *https://home.nra.org/about-the-nra/*

Elving, Ron. "The NRA Wasn't Always against Gun Restrictions." National Public Radio. October 10, 2017. *https://www.npr.org/2017/10/10/556578593/the-nra-wasnt-always-against-gun-restrictions*

Rothman, Lily. "The Original Reason the NRA Was Founded." *Time*. November 17, 2015. *http://time.com/4106381/nra-1871-history/*

Bureau of Alcohol, Tobacco, Firearms, and Explosives. "National Firearms Act" and "Title II of the Gun Control Act of 1968." *https://www.atf.gov/rules-and-regulations/national-firearms-act*

Bureau of Alcohol, Tobacco, Firearms, and Explosives. "Gun Control Act." *https://www.atf.gov/rules-and-regulations/gun-control-act*

Black Panther Party, the Mulford Act, Ronald Reagan, George H. W. Bush, Harlon Carter, Radio Lab: More Perfect – The Gun Show

Albert Duncan, Garrett. "Black Panther Party." *Encyclopaedia Britannica. https://www.britannica.com/topic/Black-Panther-Party*

History Channel. "Black Panthers." A&E Television Networks. Updated August 21, 2018. *https://www.history.com/topics/civil-rights-movement/black-panthers*

Morgan, Thad. "The NRA Supported Gun Control When the Black Panthers Had the Weapons." History Channel: History Stories. March 22, 2018. *https://www.history.com/news/black-panthers-gun-control-nra-support-mulford-act*

Weber, Peter. "How Ronald Reagan Learned to Love Gun Control." *The Week*. December 3, 2015. *https://theweek.com/articles/582926/how-ronald-reagan-learned-love-gun-control*

New York Times Archives. "Letter of Resignation Sent by (George H. W.) Bush to Rifle Association." May 11, 1995. *https://www.nytimes.com/1995/05/11/us/letter-of-resignation-sent-by-bush-to-rifle-association.html*

Smith, Laura. "The Man Responsible for the Modern NRA Killed a Hispanic Teenager, Before Becoming a Border Agent." Timeline. July 6, 2017. *https://timeline.com/harlon-carter-nra-murder-2f8227f2434f*

Achenbach, Joel, Scott Higham, and Sari Horwitz. "How NRA's True Believers Converted a Marksmanship Group into a Mighty Gun Lobby." *Washington Post*. January 12, 2013. *https://www.washingtonpost.com/politics/how-nras-true-believers-converted-a-marksmanship-group-into-a-mighty-gun-lobby/2013/01/12/51c62288-59b9-11e2-88d0-c4cf65c3ad15_story.html?utm_term=.30cb2a82270a*

Radiolab Presents: More Perfect – The Gun Show. New York Public Radio/National Public Radio. WNYC Studios, October 11, 2017.

Military Casualties, Historical Revolutions, Support of Gun Rights, the West, Tyranny

Katzenell, Udi, Nachman Ash, Ana L. Tapia, Gadi Abebe Campino, and Elon Glassberg. "Analysis of the Causes of Death of Casualties in Field Military Setting." *Military Medicine* 177 (2012): 1065–1068. doi:10.7205/MILMED-D-12-00161

Wikipedia. "List of Revolutions and Rebellions." *https://en.wikipedia.org/wiki/List_of_revolutions_and_rebellions*

Chang, Alvin. "How America Built Itself on Guns, Then Couldn't Let It Go." Vox. June 20, 2016. *https://www.vox.com/2016/6/20/11966234/america-built-guns-cant-let-go*

Secure Penguin. "Dealing with an Intruder." *http://www.securepenguin.com/dealing-with-an-intruder/*

Mosher, Dave, and Skye Gould. "How Likely Are Foreign Terrorists to Kill Americans? The Odds May Surprise You." *Business Insider*. January 31, 2017. *https://www.businessinsider.com/death-risk-statistics-terrorism-disease-accidents-2017-1*

Durisin, Megan, and Shruti Singh. "Americans Will Eat a Record Amount of Meat in 2018." Bloomberg News. January 2, 2018. *https://www.bloomberg.com/news/articles/2018-01-02/have-a-meaty-new-year-americans-will-eat-record-amount-in-2018*

Kopel, David. "Why the Anti-Tyranny Case for the 2nd Amendment Shouldn't Be Dismissed So Quickly." Vox. August 22, 2016. *https://www.vox.com/2016/8/22/12559364/second-amendment-tyranny-militia-constitution-founders*

Entitlements, Private Lender, Hard Money, Soft Money, the Fed, Entitlements

Lee, Dawn. "List of 80+ Federal Welfare Programs." Single Mother Guide. Updated July 3, 2018. *https://singlemother-guide.com/federal-welfare-programs/*

USA.gov. "Government Benefits." *https://www.usa.gov/benefits*

Cogan, John F. *The High Cost of Good Intentions: A History of U.S. Federal Entitlement Programs.* Stanford University Press, 2017.

Cambridge Dictionary. "Private Lender." *https://dictionary.cambridge.org/us/dictionary/english/private-lender*

Investopedia. "Hard Money Loan." *https://www.investopedia.com/terms/h/hard_money_loan.asp*

Investopedia. "Soft Loan." *https://www.investopedia.com/terms/s/softloan.asp*

Lake, Rebecca. "Using Hard Money Loans for Real Estate Investments." Investopedia. September 1, 2017. *https://www.investopedia.com/articles/wealth-management/040216/using-hard-money-loans-real-estate-investments.asp*

Federal Reserve Education. "The Structure and Functions of the Federal Reserve." *https://www.federalreserveeducation.org/about-the-fed/structure-and-functions*

Obringer, Lee Ann. "How the Fed Works." How Stuff Works. *https://money.howstuffworks.com/fed.htm*

Investopedia. "The Federal Reserve: What Is the Fed?" *https://www.investopedia.com/university/thefed/fed1.asp*

Socialism, Capitalism, Fed Funds Rate, Ben Bernanke and GSE Conservatorships, Bailouts

Cambridge Dictionary. "Socialism." *https://dictionary.cambridge.org/us/dictionary/english/socialism*

Dictionary.com "Socialism." *https://www.dictionary.com/browse/socialism*

Dictionary.com. "Capitalism." *https://www.dictionary.com/browse/capitalism?s=t*

Macrotrends. "Federal Funds Rate—62 Year History." *https://www.macrotrends.net/2015/fed-funds-rate-historical-chart*

Federal Reserve. "Statement Made by Chairman Bernanke on Fannie Mae and Freddie Mac." Press release, September 7, 2008. *https://www.federalreserve.gov/newsevents/pressreleases/other20080907a.htm*

Haynie, Ron. "Continuing GSE Conservatorship Is a Bad Deal for Taxpayers." National Mortgage News: Opinion. September 14, 2018. *https://www.nationalmortgagenews.com/opinion/continuing-gse-conservatorship-is-a-bad-deal-for-taxpayers*

Carney, John. "The Size of the Bank Bailout: $29 Trillion." CNBC. December 14, 2011. *https://www.cnbc.com/id/45674390*

Adam Michnik, Insurance Agencies, U.S. Constitution, Calvin Coolidge, Lost Decades

Hitchens, Christopher. *Letters to a Young Contrarian*. Basic Books, 2001.

Davis, Craig. "Why Do Insurance Companies Advertise So Much?" The Content Strategist. February 6, 2017. *https://contently.com/2017/02/06/insurance-advertising-abundance/*

Preamble to the U.S. Constitution. *https://www.usconstitution.net/xconst_preamble.html*

History Central. "Calvin Coolidge." *https://www.historycentral.com/Bio/presidents/coolidge.html*

Cassidy, John. "Four Lost Decades: Why American Politics Is All Messed Up." *The New Yorker*. September 17, 2013. *https://www.newyorker.com/news/john-cassidy/four-lost-decades-why-american-politics-is-all-messed-up*

Economic Privatization, Classifying Income, Tax Definitions, the One Percent Infatuation

Buchheit, Paul. "8 Ways Privatization Has Failed America." Common Dreams. August 5, 2013. *https://www.commondreams.org/views/2013/08/05/8-ways-privatization-has-failed-america*

Kinney, Jen. "Examples of How City Services Privatization Leads to Inequality Are Piling Up." Next City. September 29, 2016. *https://nextcity.org/daily/entry/privatization-water-utilities-inequality-poverty*

Gould, Skye, and Daniel Brown. "Here's How Many US Troops and Private Contractors Have Been Sent to Afghanistan." Business Insider. August 22, 2017. *https://www.businessinsider.com/this-is-how-many-private-contractors-and-us-troops-are-in-afghanistan-2017-8*

Sentencing Project. "Private Prisons in the United States." August 2, 2018. *https://www.sentencingproject.org/publications/private-prisons-united-states/*

Agrawal, Nina. "There's More than the CIA and FBI: The 17 Agencies That Make Up the U.S. Intelligence Community." *Los Angeles Times*. January 17, 2017. *http://www.latimes.com/nation/la-na-17-intelligence-agencies-20170112-story.html*

Marquit, Miranda. "How the IRS Classifies Your Income." Wallethub. August 1, 2012. *https://wallethub.com/blog/types-of-income/372/*

Investopedia. "What Is the Difference Between Income Tax and Capital Gains Tax?" May 2018. *https://www.investopedia.com/ask/answers/052015/what-difference-between-income-tax-and-capital-gains-tax.asp*

Weissmann, Jordan. "Actually, the 1 Percent Are Still the Problem." *Slate*. May 18, 2018. *https://slate.com/business/2018/05/forget-the-atlantics-9-9-percent-the-1-percent-are-still-the-problem.html*

Tax Loopholes, RIAs, Passive, Abigail Johnson, Giancarlo Stanton, Franz Kafka

McArdle, Megan. "Those Tax Loopholes Were Created for a Reason." Bloomberg News: Opinion. April 11, 2016. *https://www.bloomberg.com/opinion/articles/2016-04-11/those-tax-loopholes-were-created-for-a-reason*

Barnes, Ryan. "What Is a Registered Investment Advisor?" Investopedia. Updated March 23, 2018. *https://www.investopedia.com/articles/financialcareers/06/whatisaria.asp*

Google Dictionary. "Passive." *https://www.google.com/search?q=passive+definition&rlz=1C1CHBF_enUS744US744&oq=passive+defi&aqs=chrome.0.0j69i60j69i57j0l3.3911j1j7&sourceid=chrome&ie=UTF-8*

Forbes. "*Forbes* 400, 2018. Abigail Johnson, #28." *https://www.forbes.com/profile/abigail-johnson/#4beafa841c42*

Sportrac. Giancarlo Stanton contract details. *https://www.spotrac.com/mlb/new-york-yankees/giancarlo-stanton-6864/*

BrainyQuote. "Franz Kafka Quotes." *https://www.brainyquote.com/quotes/franz_kafka_134853*

CHAPTER 4

Socrates, Living Generation List and Traits, Hitler, Rock Around the Clock, Oppression

Why Do We Do It! "Quote by Socrates…Or is It?" August 28, 2013. *http://whywedoit.net/blog/2013/08/28/quote-by-socrates-or-is-it/*

Novak, Jill. "The Six Living Generations in America." Marketing Teacher. *http://www.marketingteacher.com/the-six-living-generations-in-america/*

Biography. "Adolf Hitler." A&E Television Networks. Updated May 21, 2018. *https://www.biography.com/people/adolf-hitler-9340144*

Stanley, Bob. "Bill Haley: Rock Around the Clock—the World's First Rock Anthem." *The Guardian* (Manchester). May 22, 2014. *https://www.theguardian.com/music/2014/may/22/bill-haley-rock-around-the-clock-worlds-first-rock-anthem*

Meyerson, Collier. "It's Time for Americans to Reckon with the True History of Racial Oppression in This Country." *The Nation*. June 11, 2018. *https://www.thenation.com/article/time-americans-reckon-true-history-racial-oppression-country/*

Corlett, Adam. "As Time Goes By: Shifting Incomes and Inequality Between and Within Generations." Intergen Commission. February 2017. *https://www.intergencommission.org/wp-content/uploads/2017/02/IC-intra-gen.pdf*

Varying Generation Timelines, ARPANET, Tim Berners-Lee, Johannes Gutenberg

Serafino, Jay. "New Guidelines Redefine Birth Years for Millennials, Gen-X, and 'Post-Millennials.'" Mental Floss. March 1,

2018. *http://mentalfloss.com/article/533632/new-guidelines-redefine-birth-years-millennials-gen-x-and-post-millennials*

The Conversation. "How the Internet Was Born: From the ARPANET to the Internet." November 2, 2016. *https://theconversation.com/how-the-internet-was-born-from-the-arpanet-to-the-internet-68072*

Brooke, Katrina. "'I Was Devastated' Tim Berners-Lee, the Man Who Created the World-Wide Web Has Some Regrets." *Vanity Fair*. August 2018. *https://www.vanityfair.com/news/2018/07/the-man-who-created-the-world-wide-web-has-some-regrets*

Biography Online. "Johannes Gutenberg Biography." *https://www.biographyonline.net/business/j-gutenberg.html*

Differing Generation Names, Communal Living, Current Housing Crisis, Shangri-La

Henseler, Christine. "A Bubble Generation: The Millennials, Generation X, and Historical Amnesia." *Huffington Post*. Updated October 20, 2014. *https://www.huffingtonpost.com/christine-henseler/a-bubble-generation-the-milleni-als_b_5691564.html*

Generation X Goes Global. "Generation X in Germany." *https://www.generationxgoesglobal.com/germany.html*

Generation X Goes Global. "Generation X in Japan." *https://www.generationxgoesglobal.com/japan.html*

Strauss, Ilana E. "The Hot New Millennial Housing Trend Is a Repeat of the Middle Ages." *The Atlantic*. September 26, 2016. *https://www.theatlantic.com/business/archive/2016/09/millennial-housing-communal-living-middle-ages/501467/*

Hobbes, Michael. "America's Housing Crisis Is a Ticking Time Bomb." *Huffington Post*. Updated June 19, 2018. *https://www.*

huffingtonpost.com/entry/housing-crisis-inequality-harvard-report_us_5b27c1f1e4b056b2263c621e

Wikipedia. "Shangri-La." *https://en.wikipedia.org/wiki/Shangri-La*

Manufacturing and Service Industries, Expense of Live Events, Communication, Ovid

Long, Heather. "U.S. Has Lost 5 Million Manufacturing Jobs Since 2000." CNN Business. March 29, 2016. *https://money.cnn.com/2016/03/29/news/economy/us-manufacturing-jobs/index.html*

Desilver, Drew. "10 Facts About American Workers." Pew Research Center. September 1, 2016. *http://www.pewresearch.org/fact-tank/2016/09/01/8-facts-about-american-workers/*

Robaton, Anna. "Why So Many Americans Hate Their Jobs." CBS Money Watch. March 31, 2017. *https://www.cbsnews.com/news/why-so-many-americans-hate-their-jobs/*

Brown, Maury. "Have Concerts and Sporting Events Become Too Expensive for the Average Fan?" *Forbes*. July 23, 2014. *https://www.forbes.com/sites/maurybrown/2014/07/23/have-concerts-and-sporting-events-become-too-expensive-for-the-average-fan/#fd62ee916f72*

Iqbal, Nosheen. "Have Smartphones Killed the Art of Conversation?" *The Guardian* (Manchester). August 5, 2018. *https://www.theguardian.com/technology/2018/aug/05/smartphones-kill—art-of-conversation-voice-calls-whatsapp-emojis*

Oberoi, Rashmi. "The Dying Art of Conversation." *The Citizen*. February 24, 2017. *https://www.thecitizen.in/index.php/en/NewsDetail/index/9/10018/The-Dying-Art-of-Conversation*

QuoteFancy. "Ovid." *https://quotefancy.com/quote/9024/Ovid-Dripping-water-hollows-out-stone-not-through-force-but-through-persistence*

Smartphones, Parkland Students, Gen Z Anxiety, Opioid Epidemic, Infocalypse

Tweedie, Steven. "The World's First Smartphone, Simon, Was Created 15 Years Before the iPhone." *Business Insider*. June 14, 2015. *https://www.businessinsider.com/worlds-first-smartphone-simon-launched-before-iphone-2015-6*

Grinberg, Emanuella, and Nadeem Muaddi. "How the Parkland Students Pulled Off a Massive National Protest in Only 5 Weeks." CNN. March 26, 2018. *https://www.cnn.com/2018/03/26/us/march-for-our-lives/index.html*

Lima, Cristiano. "Companies Pull Ads from Fox's Ingraham After Her Jab at Parkland Student." *Politico*. March 29, 2018. *https://www.politico.com/story/2018/03/29/laura-ingraham-david-hogg-college-acceptance-491475*

Stillman, Jessica. "Gen Z Is Anxious, Distrustful, and Often Downright Miserable, New Poll Reveals." *Inc.* March 23, 2016. *https://www.inc.com/jessica-stillman/gen-z-is-anxious-distrustful-and-often-downright-miserable-new-poll-reveals.html*

National Institute on Drug Abuse. "Opioid Overdose Crisis." Updated March 2018. *https://www.drugabuse.gov/drugs-abuse/opioids/opioid-overdose-crisis*

Klein, Rebecca. "Teachers Are Serving as First Responders to the Opioid Crisis." *Huffington Post.* November 3, 2018. *https://www.huffingtonpost.com/entry/teachers-opioid-epidemic-drugs-children_us_5bd9c9c4e4b01abe6a1a4206?utm_medium=10today.ad1.20181105&utm_source=email&utm_content=article&utm_campaign=10-for-today—-4.0-styling*

Kundu, Kishayala. "The Infocalypse Is Upon Us, and It's Only Going to Get Worse, Says Leading Researcher."

Beebom. February 12, 2018. *https://beebom.com/infocalypse-aviv-ovadya-deepfakes-fake-news/*

Types of Schooling, Pledge of Allegiance, Public School Attendance, Budgets, Teacher Pay

Flavin, Brianna. "The Ultimate Guide to 13 Different Types of Schools Across America." Rasmussen College. July 4, 2016. *https://www.rasmussen.edu/degrees/education/blog/types-of-schools/*

Teach.com. "Types of Schools." *https://teach.com/become/where-can-i-teach/types-of-schools/*

FindLaw. "School Prayer and the Pledge of Allegiance: Background." *https://education.findlaw.com/student-rights/school-prayer-and-the-pledge-of-allegiance-background.html*

Jennings, Jack. "Proportion of U.S. Students in Private School Is 10 Percent and Declining." *Huffington Post*. Updated December 6, 2017. *https://www.huffingtonpost.com/jack-jennings/proportion-of-us-students_b_2950948.html*

Gartner, Jess. "How Are Public Schools Funded?" Allovue. October 30, 2017. *https://allovue.com/blog/2017/how-are-public-schools-funded*

National Center for Education Statistics. "Public School Revenue Sources." Updated April 2018. *https://nces.ed.gov/programs/coe/indicator_cma.asp*

New York Times Magazine. "The Education Issue." September 9, 2018. *https://www.nytimes.com/issue/magazine/2018/09/06/the-9918-issue*

Lowe, Jaime. "The Second Shift: What Teachers Are Doing to Pay Their Bills." *New York Times Magazine*. September 6, 2018. *https://www.nytimes.com/interactive/2018/09/06/magazine/teachers-america-second-jobs.html*

Worldwide School Rankings, Private School, Home School, Magnet School and Issues

Human Rights Advocate. "2017 World Best Education Systems—1st Quarter Report." World Top 20 Project. May 5, 2017. *https://worldtop20.org/2017-world-best-education-systems-1st-quarter-report*

Jackson, Abby, and Andy Kiersz. "The Latest Ranking of Top Countries in Math, Reading, and Science Is Out—and the U.S. Didn't Crack the Top 10." Business Insider. December 6, 2016. *https://www.businessinsider.com/pisa-worldwide-ranking-of-math-science-reading-skills-2016-12*

Council for American Private Education. "Facts and Studies." *http://www.capenet.org/facts.html*

Homeschool.com. "The Different Ways to Homeschool." *https://www.homeschool.com/new/difstyles.asp*

Magnet Schools of America. "What Are Magnet Schools." *http://magnet.edu/about/what-are-magnet-schools*

Waldrip, Donald. "A Brief History of Magnet Schools." Magnet Schools of America. *http://magnet.edu/brief-history-of-magnets*

Harbison, Victor. "Magnet Schools: More Harm Than Good?" *New York Times* Opinion. February 10, 2009. *https://kristof.blogs.nytimes.com/2009/02/10/magnet-schools-more-harm-than-good/*

Sparks, Sarah D. "Magnet Schools Struggle to Be Diverse, Says Study." *Education Week*. June 9, 2015. *https://www.edweek.org/ew/articles/2015/06/10/magnet-schools-struggle-to-be-diverse-says.html*

Charter Schools: Principles, History, Who Can Start One, and Issues, Tenets of Capitalism

Finn, Chester E., Jr., and Brandon L. Wright. "Where Did Charter Schools Come From?" Education Next. May 9, 2016. *https://www.educationnext.org/where-did-charter-schools-come-from/*

In Perspective. "Key Facts About Charter Schools." *http://www.in-perspective.org/pages/introduction*

Wikipedia. "Charter Schools in the United States." *https://en.wikipedia.org/wiki/Charter_schools_in_the_United_States*

Strauss, Valerie. "Why Opening a Charter School Is a Lot Like Opening Your Own Business." *Washington Post.* December 22, 2016. *https://www.washingtonpost.com/news/answer-sheet/wp/2016/12/22/under-trump-will-the-marketplace-be-the-only-regulator-of-school-choice/?utm_term=.95d728eb05c4*

Chen, Michelle. "Charter Schools Are Reshaping America's Education System for the Worse." *The Nation.* January 4, 2018. *https://www.thenation.com/article/charter-schools-are-reshaping-americas-education-system-for-the-worse/*

Dunbar, John. "The 'Citizens United' Decision and Why It Matters." Center for Public Integrity. October 18, 2012. *https://www.publicintegrity.org/2012/10/18/11527/citizens-united-decision-and-why-it-matters*

Zucchi, Kristina. "Main Characteristics of Capitalist Economies." Investopedia. Updated October 15, 2018. *https://www.investopedia.com/articles/investing/102914/main-characteristics-capitalist-economies.asp*

Online Schooling, Robert Johnson, Workforce Disruption, Four Cs of Twenty-First-Century Learning

Online Schools Center. "Getting Connected: A Brief History of Online Education." *https://www.onlineschoolscenter.com/history-of-online-education/*

Online Schools Org. "The History of Online Schooling." Visual Academy. *https://www.onlineschools.org/visual-academy/the-history-of-online-schooling/*

Peterson's. "This History of Online Education." November 29, 2017. *https://www.petersons.com/blog/the-history-of-online-education/*

Potts, Rolf. "Robert Johnson Sold His Soul to the Devil in Rosedale, Mississippi." April 16, 2004. *https://rolfpotts.com/robert-johnson-sold-his-soul-to-the-devil-in-rosedale-mississippi/*

Drum, Kevin. "You Will Lose Your Job to a Robot—and Sooner Than You Think." *Mother Jones*. November/December 2017. *https://www.motherjones.com/politics/2017/10/you-will-lose-your-job-to-a-robot-and-sooner-than-you-think/*

Chang, Sue. "This Chart Spells Out in Black and White Just How Many Jobs Will Be Lost to Robots." Market Watch. September 2, 2017. *https://www.marketwatch.com/story/this-chart-spells-out-in-black-and-white-just-how-many-jobs-will-be-lost-to-robots-2017-05-31*

National Education Association. "An Educator's Guide to the 'Four Cs': Preparing 21st Century Students for a Global Society." *http://www.nea.org/tools/52217.htm*

P21: Partnership for 21st Century Learning. *http://www.p21.org/about-us/our-mission*

P21: Partnership for 21st Century Learning. "Is It Time for a Fifth C?" *http://www.p21.org/news-events/p21blog/2289-is-it-time-for-a-fifth-c*

PowerSchool. "Connecting the Four Cs of the 21st Century Education (With a 5th C!)." March 9, 2016. *https://www.powerschool.com/resources/blog/connecting-4-cs-21st-century-education-5th-c/*

Walters, Genevra, Nicole Devries, and Jamie Harbin. "Future Forward: How to Incorporate the Fifth 'C' of 21st Century Learning" eSchool News. October 25, 2017. *https://www.eschoolnews.com/2017/10/25/future-5th-c-career-readiness/*

DeWitt, Peter. "Should There Be a 5th C in the Partnership for a 21st-Century Learning?" *Education Week*. January 8, 2017. *http://blogs.edweek.org/edweek/finding_common_ground/2017/01/should_there_be_a_5th_c_in_the_partnership_for_21st_century_learning.html*

Generation Alpha and Birth Rate, World Death Rate, India, Islam, Caucasian Representation

Michael Carter, Christine. "The Complete Guide to Generation Alpha, the Children of Millennials." *Forbes*. December 21, 2016. *https://www.forbes.com/sites/christinecarter/2016/12/21/the-complete-guide-to-generation-alpha-the-children-of-millennials/#413fb19d3623*

Mirken, Jenny. "Here Comes Generation Alpha." *Media Daily News*. October 23, 2018. *https://www.mediapost.com/publications/article/326922/here-comes-generation-alpha.html*

Mccrindle. "Gen Z and Gen Alpha Infographic Update." *https://mccrindle.com.au/insights/blogarchive/gen-z-and-gen-alpha-infographic-update/*

Lamble, Lucy. "With 250 Babies Born Each Minute, How Many People Can the Earth Sustain?" *The Guardian* (Manchester). April 23, 2018. *https://www.*

theguardian.com/global-development/2018/apr/23/population-how-many-people-can-the-earth-sustain-lucy-lamble

Bump, Philip. "What America Will Look Like in 2050, in 4 Charts." *Washington Post*. April 3, 2015. *https://www.washingtonpost.com/news/the-fix/wp/2015/04/03/what-america-will-look-like-in-2050-less-christian-less-white-more-gray/?utm_term=.343c259e08ad*

Hard Timers, Nineteenth-Century Advancements, Twentieth-Century Advancements, Scientific Revolution

Rosenberg, Matt. "Generational Names in the United States." ThoughtCo. September 21, 2018. *https://www.thoughtco.com/names-of-generations-1435472*

Danelek, Jeff. "Top 10 Greatest Inventions of the 19th Century." TopTenz. August 9, 2010. *https://www.toptenz.net/top-10-greatest-inventions-of-the-19th-century.php*

Danelek, Jeff. "Top 10 Important Inventions of the 20th Century." TopTenz. September 9, 2010. *https://www.toptenz.net/top-10-inventions-of-the-20th-century.php*

Kreis, Stevens. "Lecture 10: The Scientific Revolution, 1543–1600." History Guide. 2002. *http://www.historyguide.org/earlymod/lecture10c.html*

Copernicus, Twenty-First-Century Advancements, Oedipus Complex

BBC History. "Copernicus." *http://www.bbc.co.uk/history/historic_figures/copernicus.shtml*

CERN. "The Higgs Boson." *https://home.cern/topics/higgs-boson*

Mars One. "Human Settlement on Mars." *https://www.mars-one.com/*

Encyclopaedia Britannica. "Oedipus Complex." *https://www.britannica.com/science/Oedipus-complex*

CHAPTER 5

Introversion, Recreational Smoking, USDA Food Pyramid, HIV Misconceptions, 5G

Dictionary.com. "Introvert." *https://www.dictionary.com/browse/introvert*

Google Dictionary. "Reticent." *https://www.google.com/search?q=reticent&rlz=1C1CHBF_enUS775US775&oq=reticent&aqs=chrome..69i57j0l5.3009j1j7&sourceid=chrome&ie=UTF-8*

Urban Dictionary. "Introvert." *https://www.urbandictionary.com/define.php?term=Introvert*

Granneman, Jennifer. "Why Introverts and Extraverts Are Different: The Science." Quiet Revolution. *https://www.quietrev.com/why-introverts-and-extroverts-are-different-the-science/*

Klara, Robert. "When Doctors Prescribed 'Healthy' Cigarette Brands." *Adweek*. June 18, 2015. *https://www.adweek.com/brand-marketing/throwback-thursday-when-doctors-prescribed-healthy-cigarette-brands-165404/*

Brusie, Chaunie. "How Did the Government Get the Food Pyramid So Terribly Wrong?" Healthy Way. October 3, 2017. *https://www.healthyway.com/content/how-did-the-government-get-the-food-pyramid-so-terribly-wrong/*

Heller, Jacob. "Rumors and Realities: Making Sense of HIV/AIDS Conspiracy Narratives and Contemporary Legends." US National Library of Medicine, National Institutes of Health. January 2015. *https://www.ncbi.nlm.nih.gov/pmc/articles/PMC4265931/*

Villas-Boas, Antonio. "AT&T's and Verizon's 5G Networks Are Coming This Year, and Your Internet Speeds Will Be Insanely Fast When They Arrive." Business Insider. January 4, 2018. *https://www.businessinsider.com/5g-speed-network-lte-2018-1*

Social Media Dark Side, Foot-in-Mouth Syndrome, Pythagorean Theorem, Daydreaming

Close Scheinbaum, Angeline, and Gary Wilcox. "We All Need to Be Aware of the Dark Side of Social Media." *UT News*. June 1, 2017. *https://news.utexas.edu/2017/06/01/we-all-need-to-be-aware-of-the-dark-side-of-social-media*

Urban Dictionary. "Foot-in-Mouth Syndrome." *https://www.urbandictionary.com/define.php?term=Foot-In-Mouth%20Syndrome*

Basic Mathematics. "Pythagorean Theorem." *https://www.basic-mathematics.com/pythagorean-theorem.html*

Feldman, David B. "Why Daydreaming Is Good for Us." *Psychology Today*. December 19, 2017. *https://www.psychologytoday.com/us/blog/supersurvivors/201712/why-daydreaming-is-good-us*

Id, Ego, and Superego, Rafael Nadal 2008, the Punisher, Glengarry Glen Ross

McLeod, Saul. "Id, Ego, and Superego." Simply Psychology. Updated 2016. *https://www.simplypsychology.org/psyche.html*

Tignor, Steve. "Nadal Beats Federer in the Greatest Match of All Time." Tennis.com. December 3, 2015. *http://www.tennis.com/pro-game/2015/12/2008-nadal-beats-federer-greatest-match-all-time/56955/*

Marvel. "The Punisher." *https://www.marvel.com/characters/punisher-frank-castle*

Glengarry Glen Ross. Dir. James Foley. New Line Cinema, 1992.

Conspicuous Consumption, Thorstein Veblen, Rugged Individualism, and Ronald Reagan

Conspicuousconsumption.org. "What Is Conspicuous Consumption?" *http://www.conspicuousconsumption.org/*

Veblen, Thorstein. *The Theory of the Leisure Class: An Economic Study in the Evolution of Institutions*. Macmillan, 1899.

Merriam-Webster. "Rugged Individualism." *https://www.merriam-webster.com/dictionary/rugged%20individualism*

Cannon, Lou. "Ronald Reagan All-American Individualist." *Washington Post*. April 22, 1991. *https://www.washingtonpost.com/archive/lifestyle/1991/04/22/ronald-reagan-all-american-individualist/9fb8e00c-dbaa-4b5e-a145-2e3e268052fd/?utm_term=.0d315579ac3c*

Kinsley, Michael. "The Irony and the Ecstasy." *Vanity Fair*. January 2015. *https://www.vanityfair.com/news/2015/01/ronald-reagan-policy-political-failure*

Middle-Class Morality, U.S. Record of Consumption, Cost of Basic Necessities, Fossil Fuels

Bernard Shaw, George. *Pygmalion*. Premiered October 16, 1913. Hofburg Theatre, Vienna.

Pygmalion. Dir. Anthony Asquith and Leslie Howard. Metro-Goldwyn-Mayer, 1938.

Real Estate Conversation. "Australia No Longer Has the Biggest Houses in the World." October 31, 2016. *https://www.therealestateconversation.com.au/news/2016/10/31/australia-no-longer-has-the-biggest-houses-the-world/1477900553*

Statista. "Level of Household Appliance and Device Ownership in United States' Households as of May 2017, by Device." *https://www.statista.com/statistics/710587/united-states-statista-survey-household-device-ownership/*

Driving Zone. "America Loves Pickup Trucks: An Analysis of Vehicular Spending Across the U.S." Everycarlisted.com. March 26, 2105. *http://www.everycarlisted.com/drivingzone/features/america-loves-pickup-trucks-an-analysis-of-vehicular-spending-across-the-u-s*

Lam, Bourree. "The Surging Cost of Basic Needs." *The Atlantic*. June 2, 2016. *https://www.theatlantic.com/business/archive/2016/06/household-basic-spending/485330/*

Ingraham, Christopher. "The Stuff We Really Need Is Getting More Expensive. Other Stuff Is Getting Cheaper." *Washington Post*. August 17, 2016. *https://www.washingtonpost.com/news/wonk/wp/2016/08/17/the-stuff-we-really-need-is-getting-more-expensive-other-stuff-is-getting-cheaper/?utm_term=.1652eac58bf2*

Alden Dinan, Kinsey. "Budgeting for Basic Needs: A Struggle for Working Families." National Center for Children in Poverty. March 2009. *http://www.nccp.org/publications/pub_858.html*

Widdison, Geoffrey. "Though Ancient, Fossil Fuels Don't Actually Come from Fossils." *Forbes*. June 28, 2017. *https://www.forbes.com/sites/quora/2017/06/28/though-ancient-fossil-fuels-dont-actually-come-from-fossils/#403b38e66081*

Brookings Institute, Wage Stagnation, Median Income vs. Life Costs, Savings, How We Live

Kharas, Homi, and Kristofer Hamel. "A Global Tipping Point: Half the World Is Now Middle Class or Wealthier." Brookings. September 27, 2018. *https://www.brookings.edu/blog/future-development/2018/09/27/a-global-tipping-point-half-the-world-is-now-middle-class-or-wealthier/*

Desilver, Drew. "For Most U.S. Workers, Real Wages Have Barely Budged in Decades." Pew Research Center. August 7, 2018. *http://www.pewresearch.org/fact-tank/2018/08/07/for-most-us-workers-real-wages-have-barely-budged-for-decades/*

Kochnar, Rakesh. "The American Middle Class Is Stable in Size, But Losing Ground Financially to Upper-Income Families." Pew Research Center. September 6, 2018. *http://www.pewresearch.org/fact-tank/2018/09/06/the-american-middle-class-is-stable-in-size-but-losing-ground-financially-to-upper-income-families/*

Maranjian, Selena. "7 Common Expenses Growing Much Faster Than Inflation." CNN Money. August 4, 2017. *https://money.cnn.com/2017/08/02/pf/expenses-inflation/index.html*

Martin, Emmie. "Here's How Much More Expensive Life Is for You Than It Was for Your Parents." CNBC Money. June 21, 2017. *https://www.cnbc.com/2017/06/21/life-is-much-more-expensive-for-you-than-it-was-for-your-parents.html*

Spross, Jeff. "The American Savings Crisis, Explained." *The Week*. December 7, 2017. *https://theweek.com/articles/741727/american-savings-crisis-explained*

Dickler, Jessica. "Most Americans Live Paycheck to Paycheck." CNBC. August 24, 2017. *https://www.cnbc.com/2017/08/24/most-americans-live-paycheck-to-paycheck.html*

Gabler, Neal. "The Secret Shame of Middle-Class Americans." *The Atlantic*. May 2016 Issue. *https://www.theatlantic.com/magazine/archive/2016/05/my-secret-shame/476415/*

History. "National Debt." A&E Networks Television. Updated August 21, 2018. *https://www.history.com/topics/us-government/national-debt*

War of the Worlds, Churchill, Human Nature, Nature vs. Nurture

The War of the Worlds. Dir. Byron Haskin. Paramount Pictures, 1953.

Phrase Finder. "The Meaning and Origin of a Riddle Wrapped Up in an Enigma." *https://www.phrases.org.uk/meanings/31000.html*

Encyclopaedia Britannica. "Human Nature." *https://www.britannica.com/topic/human-nature*

McLeod, Saul. "Nature vs. Nurture in Psychology." Simply Psychology. Updated 2017. *https://www.simplypsychology.org/naturevsnurture.html*

Bin Laden Celebration, Incarceration, Immigrant Detentions, Japanese Internment Camps

YouTube. "The Death of Osama Bin Laden." May 1, 2011. *https://www.youtube.com/watch?v=ZNYmK19-d0U*

YouTube. "Crowd Celebrates Death of Osama Bin Laden." May 1, 2011. *https://www.youtube.com/watch?v=-FmHti8iBQM*

Roth, Alisa. *Insane: America's Criminal Treatment of Mental Illness.* Basic Books, 2018.

Haberman, Clyde. "For Private Prisons, Detaining Immigrants Is Big Business." *New York Times.* October 1, 2018. *https://www.nytimes.com/2018/10/01/us/prisons-immigration-detention.html*

Fleishman, Glenn. "A Record-High 12,800 Immigrant Children Are Currently Being Detained by the U.S. Government, Report Says." Fortune. September 13, 2018. *http://fortune.com/2018/09/12/record-number-immigrant-children-in-detention/*

History Channel. "Japanese Internment Camps." A&E Television Networks. Updated August 21, 2018. *https://www.history.com/topics/world-war-ii/japanese-american-relocation*

Silicon Valley Invention Volume, R&D Output Percentages, Researchers per Capita

Silicon Valley Indicators. "Parent Registrations." U.S. Patent and Trademark Office. *https://siliconvalleyindicators.org/data/economy/innovation-entrepreneurship/patent-registrations/silicon-valley-and-san-francisco-share-of-california-and-u-s-patents/*

Organization of Economic Co-Operation and Development. "Research and Development Statistics: Human and Financial Resources Devoted to R&D, 2016." *http://www.oecd.org/innovation/inno/researchanddevelopmentstatisticsrds.htm*

ChartsBin. "Number of Researchers per Million Inhabitants per Country." Updated 2011. *http://chartsbin.com/view/1124*

Military Spending, Peace, Infrastructure Expenditures, Commitment to Renewable Energy

McCarthy, Niall. "The Top 15 Countries for Military Expenditure in 2016." *Forbes*. April 24, 2017. *https://www.forbes.com/sites/niallmccarthy/2017/04/24/the-top-15-countries-for-military-expenditure-in-2016-infographic/#5e77820b43f3*

Watts, Stephen, Bryan Frederick, Jennifer Kavanagh, Angela O'Mahony, Thomas S. Szayna, Matthew Lane, Alexander Stephenson, and Colin P. Clarke. "A More Peaceful World?" Rand Corporation, 2007. *https://www.rand.org/pubs/research_reports/RR1177.html*

Davis, Jeff. "The 70-Year Trend in Federal Infrastructure Spending." Center for Transportation. May 12, 2016. *https://www.enotrans.org/article/70-year-trend-federal-infrastructure-spending/*

Chow, Lorraine. "Minneapolis Becomes 65th City to Adopt 100% Renewables Goal." April 30, 2018. *https://www.ecowatch.com/minneapolis-renewable-energy-2564693137.html*

Reference. "How Many Cities Are There in the United States?" *https://www.reference.com/geography/many-cities-united-states-cfb3be08284e6a62*

Free Will, Genghis Kahn, Destroy, Interviews, Star Trek, Churchill Human Rights Abuses

Cave, Stephen. "There's No Such Thing as Free Will." *The Atlantic*. June 2016. *https://www.theatlantic.com/magazine/archive/2016/06/theres-no-such-thing-as-free-will/480750/*

History Channel. "Genghis Khan." A&E Television Networks. Updated September 20, 2018. *https://www.history.com/topics/china/genghis-khan*

Google Dictionary. "Destroy." *https://www.google.com/search?q=definition+of+destroy&rlz=1C1CHBF_enUS744US744&oq=definition+of+destroy&aqs=-chrome..69i57j0l5.3686j1j7&sourceid=chrome&ie=UTF-8*

Ryan, Liz. "Seven Things Never, Ever to Say in a Job Interview." *Forbes*. May 26, 2017. *https://www.forbes.com/sites/lizryan/2017/05/26/seven-things-never-ever-to-say-in-a-job-interview/#6bf18bfa4665*

Star Trek. Paramount Television. 1966. *http://www.startrek.com/*

Hari, Johann. "Not His Finest Hour: The Dark Side of Winston Churchill." *The Independent* (London). October 28, 2010. *https://www.independent.co.uk/news/uk/politics/not-his-finest-hour-the-dark-side-of-winston-churchill-2118317.html*

CHAPTER 6

White Guilt, Forgoing Status, Harrison, New York, Cherry Creek High School, Indiana U.

Strayed, Cheryl, and Steve Almond. "How Can I Cure My White Guilt?" *New York Times*. August 14, 2018. *https://www.nytimes.com/2018/08/14/style/white-guilt-privilege.html*

Bazelon, Emily. "White People Are Noticing Something New: Their Own Whiteness." *New York Times Magazine*. June 13, 2018. *https://www.nytimes.com/2018/06/13/magazine/white-people-are-noticing-something-new-their-own-whiteness.html*

City-Data. "Harrison, New York." *http://www.city-data.com/city/Harrison-New-York.html*

Public School Review. "Cherry Creek High School." *https://www.publicschoolreview.com/cherry-creek-high-school-profile*

College Data. "Indiana University Bloomington." *https://www.collegedata.com/cs/data/college/college_pg01_tmpl.jhtml?schoolId=815*

Scandal, ZBT Ouster from Greek System, Noam Chomsky, Johnny Storm Fervor

Google Dictionary. "Scandal." *https://www.google.com/search?q=definition+of+scandal&rlz=1C1CHBF_enUS744US744&oq=definition+of+scandal&aqs=-chrome..69i57j0l5.3553j0j7&sourceid=chrome&ie=UTF-8*

"Indiana University Demands Ouster of ZBT University." *Chicago Tribune*. October 21, 1997. *https://www.chicagotribune.com/news/ct-xpm-1997-10-21-9710220301-story.html*

Goodreads. "Noam Chomsky, The Common Good." *https://www.goodreads.com/quotes/15454-the-smart-way-to-keep-people-passive-and-obedient-is*

Karlin, Lily. "Michael B. Jordan Responds to Trolls Saying a Black Man Can't Play Johnny Storm." *Huffington Post.* May 23, 2015. *https://www.huffingtonpost.com/2015/05/23/michael-b-jordan-responds-trolls_n_7428500.html*

More Female Protagonists and Nonwhite Hollywood Content, Equalized Pay, Dethroning

McNary, Dave. "Hollywood Diversity Shows Some Gains but Falls Short in Most Areas (Study)." *Variety.* February 27, 2018. *https://variety.com/2018/film/news/hollywood-diversity-falls-short-ucla-report-1202711370/*

Mumford, Gwilym. "Hollywood Still Excludes Women, Ethnic Minorities, LGBT and Disabled People, Says Report." *The Guardian* (Manchester). August 1, 2017. *https://www.theguardian.com/film/2017/aug/01/hollywood-film-women-lgbt-hispanic-disabled-people-diversity*

Rose, Lacy. "The Hard Truth About Hollywood's Gender Pay Gap: Optics vs. Reality." *Hollywood Reporter.* January 17, 2018. *https://www.hollywoodreporter.com/news/hard-truth-hollywoods-gender-pay-gap-optics-reality-1075056*

Almukhtar, Sarah, Michael Gold, and Larry Buchanan. "After Weinstein: 71 Men Accused of Sexual Misconduct and Their Fall from Power." *New York Times.* Updated February 8, 2018. *https://www.nytimes.com/interactive/2017/11/10/us/men-accused-sexual-misconduct-weinstein.html*

Fantastic Four, Part 2, Juneteenth, Google Dates, The Week, Colin Kaepernick

Fantastic Four: Rise of the Silver Surfer. Dir. Tim Story. 20th Century Fox, 2007.

Juneteenth. *http://www.juneteenth.com/history.htm*

August 26, 2016: *https://goo.gl/N2VDFP*

August 27, 2016: *https://goo.gl/7MqfQP*

August 28, 2016: *https://goo.gl/FdzLNS*

Kristian, Bonnie. "10 Things You Need to Know Today: August 28, 2016." *The Week. https://theweek.com/10things/638540/10-things-need-know-today-august-28-2016*

Wyche, Steve. "Colin Kaepernick Explains Why He Sat for the National Anthem." NFL.com. August 28, 2016. *http://www.nfl.com/news/story/0ap3000000691077/article/colin-kaepernick-explains-why-he-sat-during-national-anthem*

Coaston, Jane. "Nike Reignited the Kaepernick Controversy in Naming Him the Face of 'Just Do It.'" Vox. September 4, 2018. *https://www.vox.com/2018/9/4/17818162/nike-kaepernick-controversy-face-of-just-do-it*

Spratt, Ben. "Colin Kaepernick Will Be Remembered Like Ali and Rosa Parks, Says Osi Umenyiora." *Sporting News*. September 6, 2018. *http://www.sportingnews.com/us/nfl/news/colin-kaepernick-nike-ad-muhammed-ali-rosa-parks-osi-umenyiora/1lzdo7nv0wn1k1woo662edtkcp*

Police Killing African Americans, Racism, Prison Profit, Redlining

Lowery, Wesley. "Police Are Still Killing Black People. Why Isn't It News Anymore?" *Washington Post*. March 16, 2018. *https://www.washingtonpost.com/outlook/police-are-still-killing-black-people-why-isnt-it-news-anymore/2018/03/12/df004124-22ef-11e8-badd-7c9f29a55815_story.html?utm_term=.75339e988dec*

Google Dictionary. "Racism." *https://www.google.com/search?q=definition+of+racism&rlz=1C1CHBF_enU-*

S744US744&oq=definition+of+racism&aqs=-chrome..69i57j0l5.3424j1j7&sourceid=chrome&ie=UTF-8

Bauer, Shane. *American Prison: A Reporter's Undercover Journey into the Business of Punishment.* Penguin, 2018.

Jan, Tracy. "Redlining Was Banned 50 Years Ago. It's Still Hurting Minorities Today." *Washington Post.* March 28, 2018. *https://www.washingtonpost.com/news/wonk/wp/2018/03/28/redlining-was-banned-50-years-ago-its-still-hurting-minorities-today/?utm_term=.5caca0d1a4d7*

Richter Scale, SCOTUS, Harvey Weinstein, Alice Walker

Cosmoquest Forum. October 2006. *https://forum.cosmoquest.org/archive/index.php/t-47919.html*

Roeder, Oliver. "Supreme Court Confirmation Hearings Have More Questions and Fewer Answers Than Ever Before." FiveThirtyEight. September 4, 2018. *https://fivethirtyeight.com/features/supreme-court-confirmation-hearings-have-more-questions-and-fewer-answers-than-ever-before/*

BBC News. "Harvey Weinstein Timeline: How the Scandal Unfolded." September 19, 2018. *https://www.bbc.com/news/entertainment-arts-41594672*

BrainyQuote. "Alice Walker." *https://www.brainyquote.com/quotes/alice_walker_385241*

CHAPTER 7

Luddites, Pride, GAFA, Four Horsemen of Infocalypse, Sneakers, FAANG, Disney, Netflix

Google Dictionary. "Luddite." *https://www.google.com/search?q=what+is+a+luddite&rlz=1C1CHBF_enU-S744US744&oq=what+is+a+luddite&aqs=-chrome..69i57j0l5.2209j0j7&sourceid=chrome&ie=UTF-8*

Encyclopaedia Britannica. "Seven Deadly Sins." *https://www.britannica.com/topic/seven-deadly-sins*

Statista. "Google, Apple, Facebook, and Amazon (GAFA)—Statistics and Facts." *https://www.statista.com/topics/4213/google-apple-facebook-and-amazon-gafa/*

Semantic Scholar. "Four Horsemen of the Infocalypse." *https://www.semanticscholar.org/topic/Four-Horsemen-of-the-Infocalypse/4460286*

Sneakers. Dir. Phil Alden Robinson. Universal Pictures, 1992.

Rapacon, Stacy. "What the Heck are FAANG Stocks? A Beginners Guide." MarketWatch. July 17, 2018. *https://www.marketwatch.com/story/what-the-heck-are-faang-stocks-a-beginners-guide-2018-07-17*

Wikipedia. "The Walt Disney Company." *https://en.wikipedia.org/wiki/The_Walt_Disney_Company*

Wikipedia. "Netflix." *https://en.wikipedia.org/wiki/Netflix*

La Monica, Paul R. "For a Moment, Netflix Was Worth More Than Disney." CNN Business. May 24, 2018. *https://money.cnn.com/2018/05/24/investing/netflix-disney-comcast-market-value/index.html*

Facebook, Social Media and Users, Social Media Dark Side, Cambridge Analytica, Oppression

Wikipedia. "Facebook." *https://en.wikipedia.org/wiki/Facebook*

Statista. "Most Popular Social Networks Worldwide as of October 2018, Ranked by Number of Active Users (in Millions)." *https://www.statista.com/statistics/272014/global-social-networks-ranked-by-number-of-users/*

Close Scheinbaum, Angeline, ed. *The Dark Side of Social Media: A Consumer Psychology Perspective*. Routledge, 2017.

The Conversation. "On Social Media, ISIS Uses Fantastical Propaganda to Recruit Members." December 4, 2017. *https://theconversation.com/on-social-media-isis-uses-fantastical-propaganda-to-recruit-members-86626*

Osborne, Hilary. "What Is Cambridge Analytica? The Firm at the Centre of Facebook's Data Breach." *The Guardian* (Manchester). March 18, 2018. *https://www.theguardian.com/news/2018/mar/18/what-is-cambridge-analytica-firm-at-centre-of-facebook-data-breach*

Head, Tom. "12 Types of Social Oppression." ThoughtCo. Updated April 10, 2018. *https://www.thoughtco.com/types-of-oppression-721173*

User Agreements, UN Right to Privacy, Zuckerberg, BAT, China, NSA Surveillance, Sex Tech Industry, Sexualized Androids

Hartzog, Woodrow. "User Agreements Are Betraying You." Medium. June 5, 2018. *https://medium.com/s/trustissues/user-agreements-are-betraying-you-19db7135441f*

United Nations. "United Nations General Assembly Agenda Item 68(b): The Right to Privacy in the Digital Age." *http://www.un.org/ga/search/view_doc.asp?symbol=A/C.3/71/L.39/Rev.1*

Van Buskirk, Eliot. "Report: Facebook CEO Mark Zuckerberg Doesn't Believe in Privacy." *Wired.* April 28, 2010. *https://www.wired.com/2010/04/report-facebook-ceo-mark-zuckerberg-doesnt-believe-in-privacy/*

Haskins, Caroline. "Today Zuckerberg Made It Clear He Doesn't Care About Users." The Outline. April 10, 2018. *https://theoutline.com/post/4128/mark-zuckerberg-kamala-harris-facebook-priorities-cambridge-analytica?zd=1&zi=4tj5aa57*

Investopedia. "Definition of BAT Stocks." *https://www.investopedia.com/terms/b/bat-stocks.asp*

Diamondis, Peter H. "Baidu, Alibaba, and Tencent: The Rise of China's Tech Giants." SingularityHub. August 17, 2018. *https://singularityhub.com/2018/08/17/baidu-alibaba-and-tencent-the-rise-of-chinas-tech-giants/*

Ong, Larry. "Is China Still Communist?" *Epoch Times.* Updated June 4, 2018. *https://www.theepochtimes.com/is-china-still-communist_2208716.html*

Savage, Charlie. "The NSA Triples Collection of Data from U.S. Phone Carriers." *New York Times.* May 4, 2018. *https://www.nytimes.com/2018/05/04/us/politics/nsa-surveillance-2017-annual-report.html*

Kaur, Tarandip. "Does the Growing Global Sextech Industry Have a Place in Asia?" *Forbes.* May 18, 2018. *https://www.forbes.com/sites/tarandipkaur/2018/05/18/does-the-growing-sex-tech-industry-have-a-place-in-conservative-asia/#2d5c10bcb6ed*

Braun, Liz. "SEX ROBOTS: The Future of Sex?" *Toronto Sun.* March 10, 2018. *https://torontosun.com/news/local-news/sex-robots-when-automation-meets-masturbation*

CHAPTER 8

Human Damage to Earth, Ice Ages, Mass Extinctions, Hominin Evolution, Last Ice Age

Vidal, John. "The Seven Deadly Things We're Doing to Trash the Planet." *The Guardian* (Manchester). December 19, 2016. *https://www.theguardian.com/commentisfree/2016/dec/19/seven-deadly-things-trash-planet-human-life*

History Channel. "Ice Age." A&E Television Networks. Updated August 21, 2018. *https://www.history.com/topics/pre-history/ice-age*

Pariona, Amber. "Timeline of Mass Extinction Events on Earth." WorldAtlas. Updated March 5, 2018. *https://www.worldatlas.com/articles/the-timeline-of-the-mass-extinction-events-on-earth.html*

Howard Tuttle, Russell. "Human Evolution." Encyclopaedia Britannica. *https://www.britannica.com/science/human-evolution*

Pontzer, Herman. "Overview of Hominin Evolution." Nature.com Knowledge Project. 2012. *https://www.nature.com/scitable/knowledge/library/overview-of-hominin-evolution-89010983*

Howell, Elizabeth. "How Long Have Humans Been on Earth?" Universe Today. January 19, 2015. *https://www.universetoday.com/38125/how-long-have-humans-been-on-earth/*

Zimmerman, Kim Ann. "Pleistocene Epoch: Facts About the Last Ice Age." Live Science. August 29, 2017. *https://www.livescience.com/40311-pleistocene-epoch.html*

Tectonic Plates, Supervolcanoes, Polarity Magnetism Reversal, Gulf Streams, Melting Ice Shelves, Sun Flares, Asteroid That Killed Dinosaurs, Earth's Demise in Five Billion Years

National Geographic. "Plate Tectonics." *https://www.nationalgeographic.com/science/earth/the-dynamic-earth/plate-tectonics/*

Andrews, Robin. "Here Is What a 'Supervolcano' Actually Is, and What It's Definitely Not." *Forbes.* July 23, 2018. *https://www.forbes.com/sites/robinandrews/2018/07/23/here-is-what-a-supervolcano-actually-is-and-what-its-definitely-not/#1de075764fee*

British Geological Survey. "Reversals: Magnetic Flip." GeoMag. *http://www.geomag.bgs.ac.uk/education/reversals.html*

Gyory, Joanna, Arthur J. Mariano, and Edward H. Ryan. "The Gulf Stream." *https://oceancurrents.rsmas.miami.edu/atlantic/gulf-stream.html*

National Snow & Ice Data Center. "SOTC: Ice Shelves." Updated June 22, 2018. *https://nsidc.org/cryosphere/sotc/ice-shelves.html*

NASA Space Place. "Sunspots and Solar Flares." Updated October 31, 2017. *https://spaceplace.nasa.gov/solar-activity/en/*

Active Wild. "How Big Was the Asteroid That Killed the Dinosaurs?" Dinosaur Information. August 29, 2016. *https://www.activewild.com/how-big-was-the-asteroid-that-killed-the-dinosaurs/*

Sundermier, Ali. "The Sun Will Destroy Earth a Lot Sooner Than You Might Think." *The Independent* (London). January 19, 2018. *https://www.independent.co.uk/news/science/earth-sun-collision-course-apocalypse-asteroids-astronomy-space-a8167506.html*

Protagonist, Human Migration, Fire, Hothouse Earth, First Airplane Flight, Moon Landing

Google Dictionary. "Protagonist." *https://www.google.com/search?q=protagonist+definition&rlz=1C1CHBF_enUS744US744&oq=protagonist+de&aqs=chrome.0.0j69i57j0l4.2897j1j7&sourceid=chrome&ie=UTF-8*

National Geographic. "Map of Human Migration." 2018 National Geographic Partners. *https://genographic.nationalgeographic.com/human-journey/*

Khan Academy. "*Homo sapiens* and Early Human Migration." *https://www.khanacademy.org/humanities/world-history/world-history-beginnings/origin-humans-early-societies/a/where-did-humans-come-from*

Scott, Andrew C. "When Did Humans Discover Fire? The Answer Depends on What You Mean By 'Discover.'" *Time.* June 1, 2018. *http://time.com/5295907/discover-fire/*

Goodell, Jeff. "Hothouse Earth Is Merely the Beginning of the End." *Rolling Stone.* August 9, 2018. *https://www.rollingstone.com/politics/politics-features/hothouse-earth-climate-change-709470/*

History Channel. "1903: First Airplane Flies." A&E Television Networks. Updated August 21, 2018. *https://www.history.com/this-day-in-history/first-airplane-flies*

CNN Library. "First Moon Landing Fast Facts." Updated July 13, 2018. *https://www.cnn.com/2013/09/15/us/moon-landing-fast-facts/index.html*

Fight or Flight, the Kardashev Scale, Michio Kaku, Carl Sagan, 0.7 Civilization

Cherry, Kendra. "How the Fight or Flight Response Works." Very Well Mind. Updated September 21, 2018. *https://www.verywellmind.com/what-is-the-fight-or-flight-response-2795194*

How Stuff Works—Stuff to Blow Your Mind with Allison Loudermilk. Podcast transcript. Stuff Media. *https://www.stufftoblowyourmind.com/podcasts/the-kardashev-scale-transcript.htm*

Creighton, Jolene. "The Kardashev Scale—Type I, II, III, IV, V Civilization." Futurism. July 19, 2014. *https://futurism.com/the-kardashev-scale-type-i-ii-iii-iv-v-civilization*

Wikipedia. "Kardashev Scale." *https://en.wikipedia.org/wiki/Kardashev_scale*

Biography. "Michio Kaku." A&E Television Networks. Updated April 2, 2014. *https://www.biography.com/people/michio-kaku-21429817*

Biography. "Carl Sagan." A&E Television Networks. Updated August 29, 2016. *https://www.biography.com/people/carl-sagan-9469191*

Lovell, Christopher. "Classifying Civilisations: An Introduction to the Kardashev Scale." Astrobites. March 15, 2016. *https://astrobites.org/2016/03/15/classifying-civilisations-an-introduction-to-the-kardashev-scale/*

Fusion, Antimatter, Dyson Spheres, Bitcoin, Fermi Paradox, Star Lifting, Matrioshka Brain

Fusion for Energy. "What Is Fusion?" *http://fusionforenergy.europa.eu/understandingfusion/*

CERN. "Antimatter." *https://home.cern/topics/antimatter*

Siegel, Ethan. "Dyson Spheres, the Ultimate Alien Megastructures, Are Missing from the Galaxy." *Forbes*. May 3, 2018. *https://www.forbes.com/sites/startswithabang/2018/05/03/dyson-spheres-the-ultimate-alien-megastructures-are-missing-from-the-galaxy/#7c1051913138*

Illing, Sean. "Why Bitcoin Is Bullshit, Explained by an Expert." Vox. April 11, 2018. *https://www.vox.com/conversations/2018/4/11/17206018/bitcoin-blockchain-cryptocurrency-weaver*

Siegel, Ethan. "No, We Haven't Solved the Drake Equation, the Fermi Paradox, or Whether Humans Are Alone." *Forbes*. June 26, 2018. *https://www.forbes.com/sites/startswithabang/2018/06/26/no-we-cannot-know-whether-humans-are-alone-in-the-universe/#210214087d3b*

Wikipedia. "Star Lifting." *https://en.wikipedia.org/wiki/Star_lifting*

Curiosity Staff. "A Matrioshka Brain Is a Computer the Size of a Solar System." Curiosity. September 24, 2106. *https://*

curiosity.com/topics/a-matrioshka-brain-is-a-computer-the-size-of-a-solar-system-curiosity/

Human Life Span, Robert Oppenheimer, First A-Bomb Test, Alkaline Hydrolysis, DMV

Google Public Data. "Life Expectancy." World Bank. Updated July 6, 2018. *https://www.google.com/publicdata/explore?ds=d5bncppjof8f9_&met_y=sp_dyn_le00_in&hl=en&dl=en*

Biography. "J. Robert Oppenheimer." A&E Television Networks. Updated October 5, 2015. *https://www.biography.com/people/j-robert-oppenheimer-9429168*

Temperton, James. "'Now I Am Become Death, the Destroyer of Worlds.' The Story of Oppenheimer's Infamous Quote." *Wired*. August 9, 2017. *https://www.wired.co.uk/article/manhattan-project-robert-oppenheimer*

History. "United States Conducts First Test of the Atomic Bomb." A&E Television Networks. Updated August 21, 2018. *https://www.history.com/this-day-in-history/united-states-conducts-first-test-of-the-atomic-bomb*

Zhang, Sarah. "What Is Liquid Cremation and Why Is It Illegal?" Gizmodo. April 10, 2015. *https://gizmodo.com/what-is-liquid-cremation-and-why-is-it-illegal-1696897615*

Hamm, Catharine. "Getting a California Real ID Driver's License on the First Day It's Offered? Not a Problem." *Los Angeles Times*. January 22, 2018. *http://www.latimes.com/travel/la-tr-california-real-id-drivers-license-20180122-story.html*

Bionics, Transhumanism, Raymond Kurzweil, Law of Accelerating Returns

Encyclopaedia Britannica. "Bionics." *https://www.britannica.com/technology/bionics*

Oxford Dictionaries. "Transhumanism." *https://en.oxforddictionaries.com/definition/transhumanism*

Singh, Sarwant. "Transhumanism and the Future of Humanity: 7 Ways the World Will Change by 2030." *Forbes.* November 20, 2017. *https://www.forbes.com/sites/sarwantsingh/2017/11/20/transhumanism-and-the-future-of-humanity-seven-ways-the-world-will-change-by-2030/#446b92a87d79*

Kurzweil Accelerating Intelligence. "Ray Kurzweil Biography." Kurzweil Network. 2018. *http://www.kurzweilai.net/ray-kurzweil-biography*

Kurzweil Technologies. "A Brief Career Summary of Ray Kurzweil." 2018. *http://www.kurzweiltech.com/aboutray.html*

Kurzweil, Ray. *The Age of Intelligent Machines.* MIT Press, 1990.

Kurzweil, Ray. *The Age of Spiritual Machines.* Viking Press, 1999.

Kurzweil, Ray. "The Law of Accelerating Returns." Kurzweil Accelerating Intelligence. March 7, 2001. *http://www.kurzweilai.net/the-law-of-accelerating-returns*

Vernor Vinge, John von Neumann, the Singularity, the Singularity Is Near

Macmillan Publishers. "Vernor Vinge." *https://us.macmillan.com/author/vernorvinge/*

Vinge, Vernor. *Technological Singularity.* 1993. *https://www.frc.ri.cmu.edu/~hpm/book98/com.ch1/vinge.singularity.html*

33rd Square. "Vernor Vinge's Omni Magazine Piece." May 3, 2012. *https://www.33rdsquare.com/2012/05/vernor-vinges-omni-magazine-piece.html*

Poundstone, William. "John von Neumann: American Mathematician." *Encyclopaedia Britannica.* September 28, 2018. *https://www.britannica.com/biography/John-von-Neumann*

Kurzweil, Ray. *The Singularity Is Near: When Humans Transcend Biology.* Viking Press, 2005

AI Fear Mongering, Sundar Pichai, Current AI in Use, Robot Consciousness, Augmentation, BAT Artificial Intelligence, Beijing Social Ranking System

Kasriel, Stephane. "If We Don't Stop the AI Fearmongering We'll Have a Lot More to Fear." *Fast Company*. March 22, 2018. *https://www.fastcompany.com/40545249/if-we-dont-stop-the-a-i-fear-mongering-well-have-a-lot-more-to-fear*

Clifford, Catherine. "Google CEO: A.I. Is More Important Than Fire or Electricity." CNBC. February 1, 2018. *https://www.cnbc.com/2018/02/01/google-ceo-sundar-pichai-ai-is-more-important-than-fire-electricity.html*

Adams, R. L. "10 Powerful Examples of Artificial Intelligence in Use Today." *Forbes*. January 10, 2017. *https://www.forbes.com/sites/robertadams/2017/01/10/10-powerful-examples-of-artificial-intelligence-in-use-today/#39d8e038420d*

Azarian, Bobby. "A Neuroscientist Explains Why Artificially Intelligent Robots Will Never Have Consciousness Like Humans." Raw Story. March 31, 2016. *https://www.rawstory.com/2016/03/a-neuroscientist-explains-why-artificially-intelligent-robots-will-never-have-consciousness-like-humans/*

Mack, Eric. "Meet the People Hacking Their Bodies for Better Sex." CNET. November 15, 2018. *https://www.cnet.com/news/meet-the-grinders-hacking-their-bodies-for-better-sex/*

Tracinski, Rob. "The Future of Augmentation and Performance Enhancement." Real Clear Science. April 4, 2017. *https://www.realclearscience.com/articles/2017/04/04/the_future_of_human_augmentation_and_performance_enhancement.html*

Webb, Amy. "China Is Leading in Artificial Intelligence—and American Businesses Should Take Note." *Inc.* September 2018. *https://www.inc.com/magazine/201809/amy-webb/china-artificial-intelligence.html*

Bloomberg News. "Beijing to Judge Every Resident Based on Behavior by End of 2020." November 21, 2018. *https://www.bloomberg.com/news/articles/2018-11-21/beijing-to-judge-every-resident-based-on-behavior-by-end-of-2020*

Emmanuel Macron AI, Japan's Humanoid Drywall Robot, Boston Dynamics Robots

Olson, Parmy. "Rise of Les Machines: France's Macron Pledges $1.5 Billion to Boost AI." *Forbes.* March 29, 2018. *https://www.forbes.com/sites/parmyolson/2018/03/29/frances-macron-billion-data-sharing-ai/#7235f8c44921*

Fingas, Jon. "Humanoid Construction Robot Installs Drywall by Itself." Engadget. October 1, 2018. *https://www.engadget.com/2018/10/01/aist-humanoid-robot-installs-drywall/*

Metz, Cade. "These Robots Run, Dance and Flip. But Are They a Business?" *New York Times.* September 22, 2018. *https://www.nytimes.com/2018/09/22/technology/boston-dynamics-robots.html?login=email&auth=login-email*

CHAPTER 9

Brian Andreas, Dragons, Doomsday Predictions, Global Recession, Universal Basic Income

QuoteFancy. "Brian Andreas." *https://quotefancy.com/quote/1571872/Brian-Andreas-Anyone-can-slay-a-dragon-he-told-me-but-try-waking-up-every-morning-and*

Encyclopaedia Britannica. "Dragon: Mythological Creature." *https://www.britannica.com/topic/dragon-mythological-creature*

Cole, Rachel. "10 Failed Doomsday Predictions." *Encyclopaedia Britannica. https://www.britannica.com/list/10-failed-doomsday-predictions*

Amaro, Silvia. "The Risk of Global Recession Has 'Significantly Increased,' Strategist Warns." CNBC. July 2, 2018. *https://www.cnbc.com/2018/07/02/global-recession-risk-has-significantly-increased-strategist-warns.html*

Roubini, Nouriel, and Brunello Rosa. "We Are Due a Recession in 2020—and We Lack the Tools to Fight It." *The Guardian* (Manchester). September 13, 2018. *https://www.theguardian.com/business/2018/sep/13/recession-2020-financial-crisis-nouriel-roubini*

Annunziata, Marco. "Universal Basic Income: A Universally Bad Idea." *Forbes*. July 27, 2018. *https://www.forbes.com/sites/marcoannunziata/2018/07/27/universal-basic-income-a-universally-bad-idea/#3f7f248a3269*

Covert, Bryce. "What Money Can Buy: The Promise of Universal Basic Income—and Its Limitations." *The Nation*. August 15, 2018. *https://www.thenation.com/article/the-promise-of-a-universal-basic-income-and-its-limitations/*

Shortages of Important Jobs, Insect Die-Off, AI Wealth Gap, UBI Pursuit of Dreams

Harvie, Alicia. "A Looming Crisis on American Farms." Farmaid.org. April 13, 2017. *https://www.farmaid.org/issues/farm-economy-in-crisis/looming-crisis-american-farms/*

Runyon, Luke. "As Fewer Farmers Work the Land, the Small-Town Way of Life Fades." Marketplace. July 10, 2017. *https://www.marketplace.org/2017/07/10/economy/fewer-farmers-are-working-land-what-does-mean-small-towns*

Ramirez, Kelsey. "Sorry, Appraisers, You're Wrong—There Is a Shortage." Housing Wire. June 7, 2017. *https://www.housingwire.com/blogs/1-rewired/post/40362-sorry-appraisers-youre-wrong-there-is-a-shortage*

Hoak, Amy. "The Number of Real Estate Appraisers Is Falling. Here's Why You Should Care." Market Watch. November 18, 2015. *https://www.marketwatch.com/story/the-number-of-real-estate-appraisers-is-falling-heres-why-you-should-care-2015-11-18*

Gall, Peter. "The US Is Facing a Serious Shortage of Airline Pilots." CNN. July 16, 2018. *https://www.cnn.com/travel/article/airline-pilot-shortage-united-states/index.html*

Association of Medical Colleges. "New Research Shows Increasing Physician Shortages in Both Primary and Specialty Care." *AAMC News*. April 11, 2018. *https://news.aamc.org/press-releases/article/workforce_report_shortage_04112018/*

McKie, Robin. "Where Have All Our Insects Gone?" *The Guardian* (Manchester). June 17, 2018. *https://www.theguardian.com/environment/2018/jun/17/where-have-insects-gone-climate-change-population-decline*

Snow, Jackie. "Algorithms Are Making American Inequality Worse." *MIT Technology Review*. January 26,

2018. *https://www.technologyreview.com/s/610026/algorithms-are-making-american-inequality-worse/*

Simonds, Colin, and Jacquelyn Ethredge. "Why Artificial Intelligence Will Widen the Wealth Gap." *Huffington Post.* January 15, 2018. *https://www.huffingtonpost.com/entry/why-artificial-intelligence-will-widen-the-wealth-gap_us_5a5cba44e4b0a233482e0d53*

Schiller, Ben. "What Would People Do with a Basic Income? Let Them Explain in Their Own Words." *Fast Company.* June 6, 2017. *https://www.fastcompany.com/40426347/what-would-people-do-with-a-basic-income-let-them-explain-in-their-own-words*

Beneficial Technological Advancements, Climate Catastrophe and Using AI to Combat

Pew Research Center. "Workers Express More Positive Than Negative Views on the Overall Impact of Technology on Their Careers." October 3, 2017. *http://www.pewinternet.org/2017/10/04/automation-in-everyday-life/pi_2017-10-04_automation_1-02/*

Luo, Rui. "The Impact of Technological Change and Growth on the Skill Premium in Western Europe from 1300 to 1914." VOX CEPR Policy Portal. May 14, 2017. *https://voxeu.org/article/historical-impact-technology-skill-premium*

Bajpai, Prableen. "How Microsoft Is Using Artificial Intelligence to Fight Climate Change." Nasdaq. April 6, 2018. *https://www.nasdaq.com/article/how-microsoft-is-using-artificial-intelligence-to-fight-climate-change-cm944514*

Cho, Renee. "Artificial Intelligence—a Game Changer for Climate Change and the Environment." Earth Institute,

Columbia University. June 5, 2018. *https://blogs.ei.columbia.edu/2018/06/05/artificial-intelligence-climate-environment/*

Rich, Nathaniel. "Losing Earth: The Decade We Almost Stopped Climate Change." *New York Times Magazine*. August 1, 2018. *https://www.nytimes.com/interactive/2018/08/01/magazine/climate-change-losing-earth.html*

Roberts, David. "This Graphic Explains Why 2 Degrees of Global Warming Will Be Way Worse than 1.5." Vox. Updated October 7, 2018. *https://www.vox.com/energy-and-environment/2018/1/19/16908402/global-warming-2-degrees-climate-change*

House Money Effect, Irrational Optimism and Delusion, Love and Quotes on Love, John Wycliffe, Abraham Lincoln and Gettysburg Address

Investopedia. "The House Money Effect." *https://www.investopedia.com/terms/h/house-money-effect.asp*

Goldhill, Olivia. "Humans Are Born Irrational, and That Has Made Us Better Decision Makers." Quartz. March 4, 2017. *https://qz.com/922924/humans-werent-designed-to-be-rational-and-we-are-better-thinkers-for-it/*

Google Dictionary. "Love." *https://www.google.com/search?q=definition+of+love&rlz=1C1CHBF_enUS744US744&oq=definiti&aqs=chrome.0.69i59j69i61j69i57j69i59l2j0.2919j0j7&sourceid=chrome&ie=UTF-8*

"Love Is an Open Door." Anderson-Lopez, Kristen, and Robert Lopez. *Frozen.* Walt Disney Studios, 2013.

Segal, Erich. "Love means never having to say you're sorry." In *Love Story.* Harper & Row, 1970.

Virgil. "Love Conquers All." Brainy Quotes. *https://www.brainyquote.com/quotes/virgil_143028*

Buddha. "True Love Is Born from Understanding." Quote Fancy. *https://quotefancy.com/quote/39137/Buddha-True-love-is-born-from-understanding*

Stacey, John. "John Wycliffe." *Encyclopaedia Britannica. https://www.britannica.com/biography/John-Wycliffe*

Langley, James A. "Who Coined 'Government of the People, By the People, For the People?'" *Washington Post.* March 31, 2017. *https://www.washingtonpost.com/opinions/who-coined-government-of-the-people-by-the-people-for-the-people/2017/03/31/12fc465a-0fd5-11e7-aa57-2ca1b05c41b8_story.html?utm_term=.9b30eee82af4*

History. "Abraham Lincoln." A&E Television Networks. Updated September 2, 2018. *https://www.history.com/topics/us-presidents/abraham-lincoln*

Lincoln, Abraham. "The Gettysburg Address." Cornell University. *http://rmc.library.cornell.edu/gettysburg/good_cause/transcript.htm*

ABOUT THE AUTHOR

A. M. Pfeffer grew up in Westchester County, New York, and Denver, Colorado. He earned a Bachelor of Science in Marketing from Indiana University's Kelley School of Business and has lived in Los Angeles for nearly twenty years. He is at once a devoted husband and father and a ruthless recreational tennis player. In Los Angeles, he worked in the entertainment industry before starting his own real estate related businesses. This is A. M. Pfeffer's first book, and certainly not his last.

Made in the USA
San Bernardino, CA
10 February 2019